JJ Beazley

Odyssey

Copyright © 2011 by JJ Beazley

All rights reserved.

No part of this book may be reproduced, stored, or transmitted by any means—whether auditory, graphic, mechanical, or electronic—without written permission of both publisher and author, except in the case of brief excerpts used in critical articles and reviews.

Unauthorized reproduction of any part of this work is illegal and is punishable by law.

ISBN: 978-1-4477-4104-6

To
Aine
With thanks

Encounter

It was early afternoon on a damp, misty day in mid-November. The wood through which young Brendan Bradshaw walked was silent, still and cool. It smelt earthy.

Brendan was twelve years old, and had been allowed a day off school after complaining of dizziness and a headache. He had spent the morning closeted in his bedroom, idly tinkering with his collection of toys and books. By lunchtime his headache had mostly cleared and he was bored. Something was calling him. He had always felt drawn to the special sense of nature's annual slumber that accompanies the indistinct yet subtly luminous days of late autumn, and he wanted to be out among it.

The old wood was just a short walk from his house. A quick skip along the road, up the steps that led to a track between the houses, across the piece of rough ground that everyone called "the back fields," and there it was: fenced, but easily accessible to a twelve-year-old boy. He'd walked in it often, usually alone. Brendan's friends were not much given to woodland walks. They preferred the suburban streets, the arcade of shops that stood along the road in the opposite direction, and the livelier atmosphere of the city centre. Brendan's nature was less gregarious than might be expected of an average twelve-year-old. He was happy to take part in the bustle of the boyish fraternity when it suited him, and equally happy to remain apart when it didn't.

So there he was, hands in pockets, sauntering sedately among the ancient trees and drinking in the atmosphere. The peace, the stillness and the sense of engagement with something timeless reigned supreme. The rest of the world had ceased to exist. For the time being, only Brendan and nature's massive, arboreal temple were real.

He stood still for a minute and listened. The silence was punctuated every now and then by the odd tap as a broken twig or a shrivelled leaf dropped from the canopy and landed on the richly coloured carpet of fallen leaves. He heard a scurrying sound as some small animal went secretively about its business, somewhere not too far away. He speculated on the likely identity of his co-traveller, and decided it was probably a rabbit.

He walked on, wondering why the path that ran through the middle of the wood remained clear of encroaching undergrowth. He had trodden it on many occasions and had never seen anyone else use it. He supposed it might have something to do with the house that lay on the far side, the owner of which also owned the wood. He'd never been close to the house, since he'd heard that the man who lived there was unfriendly and behaved aggressively towards trespassers.

He rounded a shallow bend and stopped to look back. This was his favourite spot. It was the point at which the nearby houses were finally hidden by the trees, and the mist that turned the more distant specimens into various shades of washed out grey helped. Now he could be anywhere in the world – or even on another world. Brendan liked that.

He took a deep breath to smell the moist air and the peaty scent of leaf mould, and then turned to continue his solitary stroll. His progress was halted immediately, blocked by a ripple of alarm that shuddered through the length of his small frame.

Standing only a few yards ahead of him was a figure, the strangeness of which temporarily suspended the accustomed connection between Brendan's mind and body. The urge to flee failed to activate his legs, and the capacity for rational thought was non-existent. For several moments, or maybe a span of timelessness that defies the established expectations of temporal progression, he felt only shock and fear. His faculty for observation soon returned, however, and was mobilised by the instinct to identify the apparition in terms he could understand.

The figure was that of a tall man, dressed in a mid-grey, full length robe, with a voluminous cowl that kept his face well hidden. He stood unmoving in the middle of the path, his hands held close in front of him and gently clasped. He appeared to be staring directly at Brendan. The most singular feature of the vision was the appearance of the robe. It seemed to shimmer slightly, setting it sharply against the dull half-tones of the surrounding wood; and the colour seemed to change for just the briefest split-second, from grey to red and back again. Then it would flash orange, then yellow – and so it continued through all the colours of the spectrum.

As the initial shock subsided and his ability to reason returned, Brendan's fear heightened. He knew that a medieval abbey had once stood less than a mile distant on a site now occupied by his school. No physical remains of the old building existed, at least not above ground, but there were the inevitable stories of ghostly monks having been seen in the neighbourhood. As usual, nobody ever claimed first hand experience, and Brendan had certainly never seen anything. Until now.

He was about to turn and run, but then the figure raised its hands; not slowly, nor quickly, but with the elegance and deliberation of a dancer's movement. Brendan felt compelled to watch as two sets of pale, long fingers pushed the hood back onto the man's shoulders. Now the figure had a face. The young boy stared at it, open mouthed.

He had not yet developed sufficient judgement to guess the man's age with any certainty, but the stranger appeared to be of the same generation as his parents. His skin was pale and freckled, his eyes light blue and piercing. They seemed powerful, but Brendan perceived no threat in them. His straw coloured hair looked fine and well cut, and was arranged in a style consistent with his apparent age. And he was smiling. He walked slowly towards Brendan while the boy stood transfixed. He still felt afraid, but a pressing sense of fascination kept him from bolting.

"Good afternoon, Brendan," said the man in a voice that was deep and rich, yet warm and open hearted.

Brendan looked up into the stranger's hypnotic eyes, his spine tingling slightly and his mind awash with a mixture of awe and confusion. His quiet reply was the best he could manage in the circumstances.

"Hiya."

The stranger's smile broadened.

"You look in fine fettle, young man. Has your headache gone?"

Brendan nodded.

"Come and walk with me, then." The man stretched out his arm by way of invitation. "I'm going - let me see - that way."

His extended arm swung round and pointed along the path that ran deeper into the wood. Brendan felt a knot of apprehension rise in his throat. There was something compelling about the stranger, something that would make a refusal difficult to contemplate, but he also knew that accompanying him would transgress all the rules of common sense. He had the presence of mind to take the simplest option.

"My dad – and my mum – says I shouldn't go anywhere with strange men. Or women," he added as an afterthought.

His companion chuckled amiably.

"Very good advice," he offered, a note of mock seriousness matching the glint in his eye. "But then, am I a strange man? Well, to you I suppose I am, yes. But I'm not really, you know. I know everybody around here. In fact, I know everybody everywhere. There's not a place or a person on earth I'm not familiar with. Does that surprise you?"

Brendan was of an age to realise that not all the pronouncements of adults should be taken literally. But this one seemed earnestly meant. He thought for a second, raised his eyebrows and nodded. The stranger raised his eyebrows too, and leaned forward slightly.

"Come on then, you'll be quite safe with me. I have... what's that phrase your father's so fond of? I have 'bigger fish to fry' than you, young Brendan Bradshaw."

The tone of voice suggested a joke, but Brendan believed him. He didn't argue; he didn't even bother to wonder why he felt safe; he just did. The stranger moved off along the path and the boy hurried to keep pace with him. He felt entirely relaxed with the man, and he found his voice.

"Aren't you a ghost, then?"

"No."

"Are you the man who lives in the house over there?"

"No."

Brendan looked up at his companion with a quizzical expression.

"Who are you, then?"

The man returned his gaze, and his smile broadened again.

"Well now, who I am would be difficult to explain. If I gave you the full version, you wouldn't understand it. So I suppose I'd better start you off with some simple stuff. What did you spend your time doing this morning?"

Brendan frowned. He wondered what on earth his earlier activities could have to do with anything. This was obviously some sort of a riddle, but he quite liked riddles. He thought back to the morning he had spent idling in his bedroom.

He had lined up his toy soldiers and fired matchsticks at them from a toy cannon. Once the enemy had been soundly defeated, he had taken out his collection of cars and put them through their paces until he got bored. They were duly parked up in rows and he had turned his attention to his books, selecting one that he hadn't read for some time – a young person's guide to the Greek philosophers. He hadn't understood Plato, and Pythagoras had seemed a bit too obsessed with arithmetic. Brendan didn't like arithmetic. Socrates had been his favourite. And he remembered that he had also spent some time looking in his dressing table mirror – pulling his eyes wide to look oriental, demonstrating a range of facial expressions to amuse himself, and pulling his nose and mouth into contorted shapes in a comical attempt to recreate the character of Quasimodo he'd seen in a film. It was then that his mother had entered the room to make the bed. She had remonstrated with him for being vane.

"Look too long in the mirror," she had said, "and the Devil will appear to spit at you."

She had said it often enough, and he had never taken the warning seriously. Until now. He looked at the stranger's still-shimmering robe, and then upwards to his handsome face. The evident connection was persuasive enough. The stranger let out a deep bellow of laughter that seemed to echo from the surrounding trees. Brendan expected the birds to scatter from the noise, but nothing stirred.

"Don't worry, young man, I'm not going to spit at you. Such uncouth behaviour would hardly be in keeping with my elevated status, now would it?"

He wondered how the man could have known about the episode with the mirror – if, indeed, he had - and of his mother's warning. It briefly occurred to him that his mysterious companion might simply have had the ability to read his mind, but his imagination was consumed with an image of powerful blue eyes looking back at him from the mirror. His own eyes were wide and his mouth agape. The man obviously knew something, or else he wouldn't have posed the riddle. And Brendan's young mind still had the enviable capacity to believe in the unbelievable. Realisation had dawned on him quickly, but then it fell away again just as quickly. He felt confident in his reaction.

"Do me a favour. You're not the Devil."

"Aren't I?"

"'Course not."

"How do you know?"

Brendan frowned again.

"'Cos the Devil's got black hair and red eyes – and horns and a tail."

"Oh, I see. Well, perhaps you'd better decide for yourself who I am then."

The look in the stranger's eyes suddenly fractured Brendan's frail certainty. He saw in them something he'd never seen before. He was not yet possessed of sufficient experience even to consider, let alone attempt, any sort of analysis of the phenomenon or his reaction to it. He simply felt his mind changing again.

"Are you really the Devil?" he asked quietly, a mixture of awe and trepidation rising easily in his boyish brain.

His companion smiled again. Brendan continued.

"Did you come and find me because I looked in the mirror too long?"

The stranger stopped. He turned to Brendan and placed his hands back in their familiar, clasped position.

"Hardly. Even if I were this personage you call the Devil, do you think I would have nothing better to do than count how many seconds everybody spends looking in the mirror? But I haven't told you who I am yet, have I? I can tell you this much, though. I see the vanity in people's hearts in an instant, mirror or no mirror. That sort of thing is wholly transparent to me. But you need have no fear on that score. When you look in the mirror, you do so as all children do – to search for clues as to who they are. That's not quite the same thing. The fact is, young man, I didn't come looking for you at all. I came to find *him*."

He held out his robed arm, pointing over to the left of the track. Brendan followed the line of the man's finger.

He was surprised at how dark it had become. It confused him for a second. Only moments before, the early afternoon light had penetrated the denuded canopy easily. He wondered whether they had walked into some deep part of the wood that he had never visited before. Or had he lost track of time, and night fallen without him realising it? He felt afraid. He had never been in the wood at night before.

But that fear paled considerably next to the horror he felt when the object of the stranger's unerring finger became clear. As his eyes grew accustomed to the darkness, he saw that something was hanging from a tree branch, something that had the shape of a person but was frighteningly still and apparently lifeless. He had never seen a dead person before either, and this person was undoubtedly dead. As appalling as the gruesome sight was, the boy's gaze was held by morbid fascination. He stared at the body for some time, and then looked enquiringly at the stranger.

"Fine sight, isn't it Brendan?" he said. "There's a well known song, you know, about innocent black people being hanged from trees like that – in the old days, in America. The song refers to the bodies as 'strange fruit hanging from the poplar trees.' Rather an apt description, don't you think? Fine fruit indeed, eh?"

Brendan swallowed hard, and then asked

"Did he hang himself?"

"Yes."

"Why?"

"Don't you want to know who he is first?"

Brendan wasn't sure that he did. He shrugged his shoulders, but realised that the question had been intended to lead him, and so he felt obliged to nod.

"His name was Mr Cooper. He used to live a few streets away from you. He hurt a lot of people over the course of his short life – his wife, his children, his so-called friends, and plenty of strangers as well. He was a brutal man who took whatever he wanted and mercilessly hurt anyone who got in his way, or even so much as annoyed him. What he didn't realise was that he was gathering about himself a cloak of increasing darkness that he couldn't see with his physical eyes. It's his darkness that you see around you now. The world is full of Mr Coopers, Brendan, but you don't see their darkness any more than they do. You're only seeing it now because you're with me. Your senses are heightened and you can see things you wouldn't normally see."

"So have you come to take him to hell?" asked Brendan weakly.

"No," said the stranger with a slight chuckle. "I don't do that sort of thing. Besides, he's already in hell. He's over there, look."

The man stretched out his arm again and pointed to a spot a few yards from the hanging body. Brendan detected a movement between the trees. The image became clearer until he recognised the shape of a man stumbling among the undergrowth. As it grew clearer still, he could see the pain and fear in the man's eyes as he looked frantically from one direction to another. Sometimes he would stop and bury his face in his hands. And the noises became louder too, the sound of wailing and sobbing interspersed with garbled pleadings. Brendan looked back at the stranger.

"Is he a lost soul now?"

"No, but he thinks he is. You see Brendan, hell isn't so much a place as a state of mind. When people are living in a physical body, as you are at the moment, their eyes see the physical world around them and their minds generally think that's all there is. But when they die and leave their bodies, the physical world has no meaning any more. Then their minds look inwards, to what's inside them. If what they see is darkness, as Mr Cooper does, they think *that's* all there is too. So they become trapped – or think they are – in a place that's dark, cold and frightening."

"So why are you here, if you're not going to take Mr Cooper to hell?"

"Oh, what should we say? Let's just call it 'professional curiosity.' I think that will do for now."

Brendan looked at the hanging corpse again, and then to the animated spirit that was now kneeling and sobbing helplessly. His companion stood in silence. Eventually, he spoke.

"Come on, let's move on shall we? Leave Mr Cooper to fester in the hell he's made for himself."

"Can't you help him to get out of it?" Brendan asked, suddenly feeling sorry for the agonised Mr Cooper.

"Not my job," replied the stranger. "Why would I feel sorry for Mr Cooper? He made his own choices and created his own consequences. Now he has to live with those consequences in order to pay off the debt he built up. I'm not here to relieve him of that debt, or even to exercise compassion. That's the preserve of other beings who operate from a different angle, the ones whose job it is to take an objective interest in the fate of individuals. Neither am I here to judge or punish, for that matter. Mr Cooper is judging and punishing himself in a manner of speaking, which is how it should be. I merely observe and make the odd little adjustment here and there, if I think it advisable."

The stranger placed his hand on Brendan's back and gently moved him forward. The two walked on in silence for a while. The scene ahead of them was light again, and the boy's consciousness began to swim slightly as he considered the strangeness of his situation and the elevated nature of the personage whose company he believed he was keeping. He remembered the time when his headmaster had walked down the school corridor with him. That had impressed him too, but this was altogether more astonishing. He looked up at his companion again. The man was looking steadfastly back, his strong eyes and gentle smile seeming to hold the summation of all knowledge.

"You have questions to ask me, don't you?" he said.

Brendan nodded.

"Carry on then. Those that you are experienced enough to understand, I'll answer. The rest you'll have to wait for."

Brendan felt encouraged. Nobody had ever called him "experienced" before. He thought carefully about his image of the one that people called the Devil. He asked the most obvious one first.

"Why do you look like that? Everybody says you've got horns and a tail."

"Correction, Brendan. Everybody says *the Devil* has horns and a tail. Have I claimed to be him?"

Brendan felt confused for a second. He wasn't sure what the man had or hadn't claimed to be. But there was something about the power of his enigmatic companion, and the interest he seemed to have in things to do with darkness, that left the boy in little doubt. He had to be either the Devil or an angel – and angels definitely had wings. The man continued.

"I don't actually look like anything," he said. "I don't have a body, at least not in any form that you'd understand. In fact, you might even say I don't exist at all; but don't concern yourself with that for now. Haven't you noticed yet that I look like somebody you know, somebody you hold in high esteem?"

The realisation came suddenly to Brendan.

"My uncle Eric," he replied.

"And you like your uncle Eric, don't you. You know that he fought bravely when he was in the army, and that he is a good and upright man."

Brendan nodded.

"Right then. Let's put it this way for the present. I'm just a form of energy – like a type of electricity, you might say. What you are seeing is a projection, something you've created yourself.

"When you first became aware of my presence, the first thing you saw was a monk. That's what you expected to see because monks used to live around here and people tell stories of them being seen. Then you saw the flashing colours. That was nothing more than your heightened senses seeing the energies that are the innate stuff of all material. By the time I removed my hood, you knew that I was something - what should we say - a bit special. And so you saw the man you hold in highest esteem – your uncle Eric. Only you didn't realise it at the time because you were too caught up with fear and wonderment. And you've been too preoccupied ever since to notice."

"So why do people say you've got horns and a tail?"

The stranger tutted loudly and Brendan began to get the message. He wasn't supposed to refer to the man in those terms.

"All right," said his companion, "I'll tell you why people say that *the Devil* has horns and a tail, if you like. That story was spread many centuries ago by silly men with half-baked notions of good and evil. It suited their purposes to frighten the gullible, that's all."

Brendan attended the local church, and so the phrase "half-baked notions of good and evil" appealed to his juvenile curiosity. The obvious question popped into his mind.

"So aren't you evil then?" he asked, adding hurriedly "...whoever you are."

The man stopped and turned towards Brendan. He looked down at the boy for several seconds, seeming to be considering just how much a twelve-year-old would be capable of understanding.

"Let me see if I can explain something to you. I know you've already learned at school that heat and light are forms of energy that you can create and control. Are you with me so far?"

Brendan nodded.

"Right then. You think of cold and dark as being the opposite, don't you?"

Another nod.

"Well think again. They're not actually opposites. 'Cold' and 'dark' are simply words you use to describe a lack of heat and light. You can't create cold, you can only remove the heat so that whatever it is becomes what you *call* cold. I can see you understand that. You're a bright boy, Brendan. It's the same with good and evil. Good actually exists as energy. Evil is simply a lack of it."

"So aren't there any such things as evil people?"

"In a manner of speaking, yes. But they're just people who turn away from the good side and do dark, destructive things - like Mr Cooper. They operate on the darker side of existence, and that's where I choose to take an interest now and then. I like to see that things are working properly at that end of the spectrum; it keeps me amused. But that doesn't mean *I'm* evil. Let's just say that I'm a bit above that sort of thing.

"It isn't just people who operate on the dark side either, you know. There are many beings – evil beings, if you want to call them that – which spend their whole existence in places far denser and darker than what most humans get down to. There's one right behind you as we speak."

Brendan felt something touch the back of his neck – something so light that it could have been no more than a breath of wind. But it sent a shockwave down his spine and he swung around in alarm.

His eyes met those of a fearsome creature. They stared down at him out of a huge head that obscured the body behind it. It was a broad, smooth, black head, shaped like that of a bull but without ears or nostrils. It did have a snout, however, and out of it two sets of vicious canine teeth protruded, one set curving upwards and one downwards. Its eyes were long and narrow, like open wounds. They were a deep, fiery red, and burned into Brendan as the creature moved closer to him. Its mouth opened slowly and drops of some scarlet, viscous liquid began to fall from it. A deep growl grew steadily in volume as the hideous teeth came to within a few inches of Brendan's face. The boy was transfixed for a second, but recoiled from the smell of bad eggs and rotting meat that assaulted his nostrils. Instinctively, he hurried to the other side of his companion for protection. The stranger laughed again.

"He's one of the less frightening examples, believe it or not. You needn't worry about him though. He can't touch you - not physically, that is. His body's made of different stuff than yours. You can sense him, even smell him as you've found out, but that's as far as it goes. Of course, if you were to call him into your world – as some people do occasionally – that would be a very different matter. Try touching him."

Brendan looked with fear and alarm into the man's face. Wild horses wouldn't persuade him to move an inch towards the creature that still stared at him menacingly. But the stranger's eyes were stronger than wild horses. Brendan obeyed, slowly. His hand passed through the creature's head as though it were made of black mist. The head turned away from the boy to look at the stranger. Brendan fancied he could discern a hint of sorrow in its eyes; and then the whole apparition faded to nothing. Brendan began to shake.

"Did you find him interesting, young man?" the stranger asked, his mouth slightly curved into the enigmatic half-smile that seemed to be his trademark. "Actually, he's rather sad you know. The reason he's so aggressive towards humans is because he envies you – he envies the fact that you have the capacity to move onwards and upwards. And there are plenty a lot bigger and more fearsome than him. But don't worry, I'm sure you'll never have to encounter another one until you have the means to deal with it."

He winked. Brendan was confused and it evidently showed, for the stranger laughed another of his mighty guffaws.

"Come on, let's walk on. You've got more questions for me, I'll be bound."

They walked forward and Brendan's nervous system soon regained its composure. He remembered something his vicar had said and asked the next question.

"Reverend Dombey says witches are bad people who worship the Devil. He says they're called Satanists and I should keep well away from them."

"Yes, I know he does. I've heard him," replied the stranger dismissively. "He doesn't have a lot of experience of that sort of thing, your Reverend Dombey. Let's just say this. Witches and Satanists are two quite different creatures. Witches are just people who use forces that science hasn't found a name for yet. Some are good, some are bad. Satanists are usually rather desperate people who only *think* they're worshipping an alternative lord and master. It's just their way of rebelling against convention. Some of them are dangerous people though, so you can take the Reverend's advice as far as they are concerned.

"Of course, there are people who really do worship the dark side. All those who live their lives in the dark places are doing that. That means people who are selfish, greedy, cruel; people who seek large amounts of power and money, and don't care who they hurt or cheat or steal from in order to get it. Many of the people of great wealth and power you see on your television set every night are some of the best examples. Some of them realise it and some don't. Many of the most avid worshippers down the centuries have been self-professed men of God – religious people, or so they claimed. Hypocrisy has always ridden high in the exercise of power - religious or temporal."

Brendan hadn't fully heard the last sentence; and what he had heard he chose instinctively to ignore, since any attempt to understand it would have distracted him from the question that had already been prompted. He spoke quietly, apologetically even.

"Are you and God..? Sorry, are the Devil and God enemies?"

"That's something I wouldn't be able to answer for you at the moment. You'll need to gain a lot more experience before you can even begin to grasp that one. The relationship between good and evil isn't as clear cut as people think. It would be like asking whether the light of day and the dark of night are enemies – a bit pointless, really. Suppose everything *were* as simple as a God living in heaven and a Devil in hell, would they need to come into conflict? Contrary to what you've been told, people don't need to be tempted by evil beings. They tempt themselves through concentrating on all the wrong things. People make their own choices, you see. Some gravitate towards the light side, and some the dark. But just think on this as you get older. The dark side has limits. Total blackness is as far as you can go. The light, on the other hand, is infinite. It has no boundaries. That's why it's the only right way forward."

The two companions were silent for a while as they walked through the peaceful, vaporous stillness that surrounded them. Brendan was trying to make sense of the many things his companion had told him. He remembered many of the words, but their meaning seemed obscure here and there. He was just about to risk further complication by asking the stranger which religion was the true one, when he saw a small head pop up out of the undergrowth a little way ahead of them. He stopped instinctively. The head looked like that of a young boy, but it was very small. And the body, obscured as it was by the tangle of briars and bracken, could not have been more than a foot or two tall. The stranger stopped too, and turned to look back at Brendan.

"Who's that?" asked the boy, pointing.

The stranger didn't follow Brendan's finger, but merely chuckled again.

"He's just one of many, Brendan," the man replied, unconcerned as usual. "Look around you."

Brendan looked around. Every few feet he saw a head, a pair of heads, or a group of heads raised above the tangled green-brown mass and watching them with evident interest. There were no bodies to be seen, just handsome, small faces framed by curly dark hair. Brendan looked at the man.

"Are they fairies?"

"If that's what you want to call them."

"Do they live here?"

"Yes."

"Why haven't I ever seen them before?"

"Because their bodies are made differently from yours. There are lots of other beings sharing this world with you, but which you're completely unaware of. If you were all made the same, you see, you'd be bumping into each other. There wouldn't be room for you all. So there are different types of physical structures having energy that vibrates at different frequencies. Don't worry about that for now, you'll learn more as you get older. Suffice it to say that it enables you all to occupy the same space at the same time without getting in each other's way. Your eyes and your brain are designed only to process those things that are made in the same way as they are. That's why they can't see things that are made differently. Not, that is, unless your mind is adjusted slightly to be in tune with them. That's what's happening while you're with me."

As they walked on, Brendan continued his struggle to understand the things the stranger had been telling him. Eventually, he became tired of the effort and began idly to kick the rust brown beech leaves that covered the path. His companion looked down at him and stopped, turning the boy by his shoulders until they faced each other.

"I'm going to show you one more thing before I send you home, something you won't understand yet but which you should hold in your mind as you grow in wisdom.

"First, a few questions. Do you think I'm real?" Brendan nodded. "Do you think Mr Cooper is real?" Brendan nodded again. "And the demon and fairies, were they real?" Another nod. "Are you real?"

The final question seemed like a test, and Brendan felt defensive. He thought for a moment, but didn't know what he was supposed to be considering. Eventually he frowned and said "Of course."

"Right then, close your eyes. Not too tight, mind. Now, listen as hard as you can."

The boy listened intensely and waited. He heard nothing. There was no breath of wind, no clattering of leaves, no scurrying of animals in the undergrowth. The world was empty of everything but his own awareness. He felt that something was settling inside him. He felt calm, warm and happy. Greatest of all, he suddenly felt possessed of infinite wisdom and maturity. He stopped breathing.

The sensation lasted only a second or two, and then Brendan became Brendan again. He felt alone and frightened. His breath returned in heavy bursts. He opened his eyes, fearing that he had been abandoned in a world he didn't understand. He was relieved to see the stranger still smiling at him. A shrivelled leaf fell at his feet and clattered loudly. He stared, questioningly but silently, into the man's face.

"I asked you whether you believed that what I had shown you was real; whether the world around you was real; whether Brendan Bradshaw was real. Well, they are, but only up to a point. What did you see when you closed your eyes?"

"Nothing," replied the boy.

"What did you hear?"

"Nothing."

"And what did you feel?"

The young, worldly Brendan lacked the means to articulate the strange sensation he had felt during his brief reverie. The best he could manage was

"That everything was OK."

"Congratulations, Brendan. You just had a glimpse of the only thing that's truly real. Put that thought away for now, but don't lose it. You'll need to remember it again one day. Come on, let's be getting you home, shall we? I think you've had quite enough learning for one day."

The two of them walked a few paces more and Brendan saw the houses through a gap in the trees. He recognised the spot. It was the same as the one from which he had first seen the hooded figure. How could that be? He didn't remember turning around anywhere.

"Clever trick, eh?" said the man, smiling his omniscient smile again.

They stopped by the boundary fence. The stranger extended his hand, inviting Brendan to climb over it. The boy did as he was bidden. But he wasn't quite ready to go home yet. He still wanted to know who the man was, and asked the question directly.

"It doesn't matter who I am, Brendan. I'm not really anybody. Let's just say I've been your teacher today. But, remember this: it isn't the teachers who are important, but the lessons. And the same holds true for religion, since you never got around to asking the question."

Brendan nodded, but then another thought occurred to him.

"Will Mr Cooper stay in his dark place forever?"

"No. He'll be helped back to a lighter place when the time's right, when he's learned a lesson or two of his own. Being human, alive or dead, is all about learning lessons, you know. Time to go home, young man."

Brendan nodded again and began to turn away. But he still had one more question to ask.

"Will I ever see you again?"

"Oh, I should think so; but I'll look different next time. We met by chance today, but I've decided you're worth taking an interest in. Off you go, now. Home!"

Brendan did as he was told. He looked back once, hoping to wave goodbye. He was not surprised to see that the wood appeared empty of everything but misty, half naked trees and ragged undergrowth. He walked home quickly, worried that he might have been out a long time and his mother be getting concerned.

He entered the house via the kitchen door. His mother was filling the kettle to make a pot of tea.

"Back so soon, Brendan?"

"Eh?"

"Did you change your mind? You've only just gone through the door."

Brendan felt confused and frowned quizzically. He said nothing, feeling there was nothing he could say to her in the circumstances. He was old enough to realise that she would put his experience down to nothing more than a childish fancy. He turned and walked through the hallway.

"Some bloody door!" he said.

"I beg your pardon, Brendan!"

Brendan didn't reply. He hurried around the corner of the stairs, purposefully avoiding the large mirror that hung close to the front door. He went up to his bedroom and threw himself onto the bed.

As he lay there staring at the ceiling, a palpable thrill of excitement rippled down the length of his body. So strong was it that it made him shiver slightly. His mind was awash with the memory of his afternoon's adventure, and he tried valiantly to remember every word the stranger had said to him.

But the big question remained: who was the man whose company he had been so privileged to keep? His earlier certainty had disappeared again. Too much of what the imposing and unworldly figure had said to him didn't fit in with such a simplistic notion. He lay still, pondering the question for some time. Eventually, he fell to considering whether a set of wings could be concealed under a monk's habit. And then he thought he head a voice whisper close to his ear.

"Is that *really* the big question?" it asked quietly.

He jumped off the bed and covered his dressing table mirror with his sweater, just in case.

The Beckoning

A middle aged man stood pensively regarding the view through the sitting room window of his double fronted Edwardian house.

The day was cool for early August, and frequently punctuated by heavy, blustery showers. The patchy greys and dull whites of the marbled sky moved swiftly northwards as belts of rain crossed the shadowless, misty vista. The window faced west, and gave a view down a long-neglected garden, across a country lane that carried little traffic, and up a shallow hill opposite that was crowned with a copse of beech trees about half a mile distant. The dull green of the rough pasture land was home to a straggly bunch of summer fattening cattle. They, at least, seemed oblivious to the capricious elements, for they were grazing contentedly.

He idly regarded the state of the window frame, on which the paintwork betrayed the lack of any attention for a very long time. The woodwork throughout the house was in a similar condition, but it was the window frames that looked the most forlorn. Patches of loose and flaking paint were augmented by black mould stains induced by years of condensation and neglect. They matched his mood. So did the view beyond the window. For the moment the rain had stopped, but its legacy was much in evidence. Everything in the garden dripped dejectedly, the grass on both lawns looked waterlogged, and the broken stone path that ran between them gleamed in the dull light of a damp and dreary afternoon.

Brendan Bradshaw had moved to the house two months earlier. Despite its dilapidated condition he had been attracted by its isolated setting, the nearest neighbour being a cottage almost a mile further along the lane. He'd expected it to be quiet there, and so it was. A number of substantial repairs had been needed initially, and now the first steps in the daunting task of decorating the whole house were underway. Brendan wasn't in the mood for scraping, filling and rubbing down paintwork that day. Every room was imbued with a damp chilliness, and he felt melancholy.

He looked back to the copse on top of the hill and recalled the strange light he had seen two nights earlier. Something having the appearance of a small yellow sphere had crossed the sky laterally from left to right, just above the top of the hill, and then disappeared behind the trees. In fact, it had appeared to enter the copse, for the trees glowed slightly for a few seconds. Brendan had been standing in the garden at around eleven o'clock, marvelling at the starry vista of a clear, moonless night. No obvious explanation had presented itself, the object having been much larger than a shooting star and lacking the tail of a comet. Brendan's knowledge of astronomical phenomena was almost non existent, and he had assumed it to be one of the many little mysteries that the night sky presents to the ignorant observer.

The small but solid clump of slate-grey trees was holding his attention now with a strength that he found surprising. Its elevated and isolated position endowed it with an air of significance somehow, but the nature of that distinction was elusive. What he knew to be a few dozen individual trees merged into a single dull mass, silhouetted against the lightness of the sky and rendered a darker shade of hazy grey by the vaporous air. There was mystery in its solitary grandeur, and that mystery was urging Brendan's torpid mind to consider the prospect of investigation.

And yet he was uncomfortable with the idea. He felt a sense of menace, or maybe even malice, locked within the stillness of its form. Perhaps it was just a natural reluctance to enter into something having the quality of the unknowable about it. He felt a sense of recognition, though; something long past and only half remembered, something that might give reason to the strange compulsion to stare and even want to visit. He knew that the still, subtly scented space within the confines of a wood could be a powerful narcotic, and that it was capable of inducing the most realistic of images in the unwary mind. He pulled himself away and considered what he might do to lift his spirits.

Nothing worked. Neither the TV, his favourite music, nor any of the books he could find in those packing crates that were readily accessible offered any relief. He felt depressed and cold. He made a hot drink and looked out of a different window while he drank it. He made his dinner and tried to find some enthusiasm for the evening TV schedules. Eventually he took a hot bath, and then drank sufficient scotch to numb his fragile senses into a suitable state to retire for the night.

The following morning brought a welcome change in the weather. The rain had moved away eastwards, and the fresh north westerly breeze was chilly but mercifully dry. After breakfast he donned his overalls and made a start on the painting in the sitting room. He would begin with the latticed window frame, which he had already bleached and sanded. His spirits were better, lightened by the odd glimpse of pale sunshine and the reward bestowed by honest, creative endeavour. Shortly after noon he replaced the lid on the paint tin, immersed the brushes in a jar of white spirit, and made lunch. He decided that the improved weather was conducive to an afternoon walk, and decided to make the short trek up the grassy slope to investigate the copse. The improvement in his mood had convinced him that his reservations were unfounded. Woods had always attracted him, and he was sure that this would be the same as any other.

He found the hill steeper than expected, and the rough grass was pockmarked with numerous divots gouged out by the hooves of the resident cattle. He watched his footing carefully, conscious of the danger of turning an ankle with an injudicious step. The herd of beasts regarded him with evident curiosity as his breathing became gradually more laboured.

He reached the top at a point close to the copse, and was surprised to find it bounded by old post and wire fencing. He collected his breath while he looked back to his house, nestled comfortably on the far side of the lane, and then to the south where the river valley was dotted with occasional buildings of varying sizes. The wind was stronger at the higher level, and the blowing leaves hissed with the first trace of dryness that betrays the advancing state of late summer. No other sound disturbed the peace and solitude of the ridge, and Brendan stood for a few minutes, revelling in his isolation from the world of mortal man. No one else belonged here, of that he was certain. He strode over to the fence, feeling sure that its ancient pedigree and advanced state of decomposition would allow easy access somewhere along its length. He soon discovered that there were several places where a piece of old wire was broken or sagging, or where a rotting post had fallen over. He made for the nearest one and stepped into the wood.

It was apparent that the cattle didn't come in here, even though they could easily have forced an entry had they so wished. The spaces between the trees looked undisturbed, and were deeply smothered with the thick green foliage of wild garlic that he knew would have boasted a dense mass of pungent white flowers a few months earlier. He strode across the thick green carpet, now spattered with the dark stains of the turning season.

He soon felt warmer. The wind that had been so keen out on the open ridge was little more than a gentle breeze beneath the swaying, sibilant canopy. It was darker too, and the wood seemed a lot bigger than he had imagined. As he walked on, sucking in the sweet and sour scent of old woodland, he became conscious of being increasingly immersed within the denseness of a deep forest. Part of his mind recalled the foreboding he had felt the day before, and a growing sense of entrapment called out for reassurance. Brendan's rational mind quelled the troublesome sensation quickly; it was merely the effect of relative distances. The copse was simply a lot bigger than it appeared from his house. And there could be no danger; walking in a straight line would bring him to the farther edge in no more than a matter of minutes.

And so he walked on. He searched the branches and the verdant ground for signs of life. He expected squirrels and rabbits; he expected birds – a scurrying tree creeper, perhaps, or a dashing nuthatch. There was no sign of life, and soon there was no wind. The canopy above his head looked denser than ever, and it had fallen into such a perfect state of stillness as to seem unreal. The only sound came from his boots pushing their way through the undergrowth; and when he stopped to gaze around, even that passed into memory. Now there was only silence.

The view in all directions was the same: trees, supremely still and eerily silent. His sense of entrapment welled up again, but more certainly this time. There was no appeal to reason. What sort of reason could account for walking into a sculpted world contained within a vacuum? For that was how it seemed at that moment. And yet his mind was undisturbed; there was no fear, no sense of panic, no desire to leave, no need to question, only quiet acceptance. The moment was profound, but it was also fleeting. He came to his senses again and decided to return the way he had come. But he didn't know which way he had come; the forest floor looked undisturbed in all directions. He had turned around so many times that he had no clue which way he was facing. And then he heard what sounded like voices.

They were muffled, but they were unmistakeably human; a deep man's voice counterpointing the lightness of a child's, the ebb and flow of pitch, rhythm and tone floating on the air like some primeval piece of music. It seemed to echo slightly. Brendan listened intensely, hoping to catch an identifiable word or a tone of voice that would betray the nature of the conversation. He caught neither, and walked slowly towards the source of the sound feeling intrigued and secretive. A few softly trodden steps further on, and the mystery deepened. As he moved to round one massive arboreal patriarch, he saw a clearing stretched out below him. Its sudden appearance was startling, partly because the view was unprepared and unexpected, but mainly because the richness of colour that burst upon him was in such contrast to the almost monochrome view to which his eyes had become accustomed.

The early August sun was high and shining into an amphitheatre of maybe a hundred feet in diameter, but the colour of the light was wrong. It had the heavy, deep yellow quality of a late October afternoon. A faint golden mist suffused the warm, sweetly scented air that now washed over him, and the fringes of the space were densely packed with unfamiliar flowers of blue and yellow. In the middle of this enchanted bowl lay a large pool, one end of which was decorated with a floating mass of lotus leaves. Its edges were rendered indistinct by a profusion of fresh green reeds. The water reflected the perfect blue of a cloudless sky, and large insects like dragonflies darted busily across its surface. One of them suddenly rose to the height of the canopy and hung there for several seconds, before diving vertically back and swooping across the water.

Brendan stood transfixed by the view for several minutes. He looked back to the dull browns and soiled undergrowth of the wood through which he had passed, and then turned his baffled eyes to the glade again. The scene had changed in one inexplicable particular. Two large pieces of tree trunk now lay on their sides in front of the pool; and on them, facing one another, sat two people.

The one on the far side was a man, a farmer it seemed, clad in mud spattered blue overalls and Wellington boots. He had a ruddy, weatherworn complexion, and strands of unkempt hair stood out from beneath the brim of an old cloth cap. Facing him was a small figure with long black hair, a little girl to all appearance, for she was clothed in what appeared to be a sleeveless dress coloured green and yellow. She sat motionless as her companion talked quietly to her. Even at that distance, her bearing displayed the grace and stillness of a child sitting rapt before a teacher or master storyteller.

Brendan kept himself concealed behind the capacious trunk of the beech tree and strained to hear the man's words. He caught nothing, and strained again when the child answered in her own high pitched tones. The sound of their voices was louder now that he was a mere fifty feet away, but the words still made no sense to him. He soon realised why: the language was foreign, and yet it sounded familiar.

The impression of a slow, melancholy Irish air washed over him for a moment. He realised it was the second time since entering the wood that his consciousness had drifted firmly into something not of his choosing. The sense that his mind was being directed by some external source came with it, and so did the certainty that there was magic here. He had spent the whole fifty two years of his life believing in magic, even though he had never witnessed it first hand. A thrill beyond anything he could ever have imagined coursed through him. Joy, confusion, expectation and a natural fear of the unknown rose and fell as he stared at the strange, unnatural couple sitting in a strange, unnatural landscape. But then a growing tide of familiarity began to take hold. The echo of a past encounter returned like a shock wave, and rocked him to the core.

His body shook violently from the power of some silent, internal explosion. He felt his mind expand suddenly, as though it were forcing itself against the confines of his skull. A brief spell of dizziness followed, and then a calm clarity asserted its grip. He recalled that strange episode as a child, when he had walked in a wood one day and met an enigmatic, robe-clad stranger who had shown him magical things and taught him strange lessons. He had been ill that day, and the next morning had begun the process of convincing himself that illness plays tricks with the senses and creates illusions. The ensuing years of growing through adolescence into manhood had confined the episode to the certainty of hallucination or a half-remembered dream. There had been many practical, worldly and emotional diversions to contend with and enjoy. Any notion of magical encounters sank into its proper place, and had lain slumbering there ever since.

But then he heard the man's voice loud and clear. It was a cultured English voice - deep, confident and hearty.

"Brendan, dear boy. Come down and join us."

The man was looking directly at him and beckoning. The child remained still, and kept her back to him.

Embarkation

Brendan's beleaguered senses took yet another turn. Such an unexpected thrust into direct communion with this dreamlike scenario set his body trembling. To be suddenly invited into its midst brought more thrills and confusion tumbling through a mind that was already on the verge of giving in to anything, however unbelievable. And yet it wasn't unbelievable; it was natural, right and inevitable. For a brief moment he knew that, as certainly as he knew the reality of his own existence. The moment passed and incredulity returned, but what could he do except walk tentatively into the mirage?

His breathing was shallow, held back by nervous indecision, as he stepped from behind the tree and made his way slowly down the gentle slope of the embankment and into the enchanted glade. That was the expression that kept forcing itself upon him. "Enchanted glade" sat firmly in front of his inner eye, as though that part of his mind still having its roots planted firmly in the world of paint pots, cracked paving stones and dishevelled window frames was trying to keep him sane. This wasn't real. Whatever it was, it was born of some fevered illusion. "Don't be fooled," it seemed to be urging, hopelessly.

The farmer stood up as Brendan approached. He was smiling broadly.

"Good day to you Brendan. So you're still certain of your own existence, are you? You're real and this isn't. This is just an enchanted glade, the stuff of fairy tales and fantasy films. Is that how it is?"

The farmer's words were followed by a low, friendly chuckle as he waved his hand to indicate a third piece of tree trunk, now set at the end of the other two and at right angles to them.

"Have a seat, my boy. Well met by sunlight, eh?"

Brendan had no words to offer in reply. Throughout the approach he had been staring at the stranger in honest bemusement. Now he looked at his prospective perch, and then at the little girl who still had her back towards him.

His attention was caught by a movement, and he saw that a wild rabbit was regarding him with great interest over her right shoulder. Its nose twitched constantly, and its long ears flicked back and forth alternately. He looked back at his jovial host as he moved across to the tree trunk. He sat down and the man followed suit.

Only now did the girl half turn her head towards him, completing the inspection with a further turn of her eyes. They were Gaelic eyes: sapphire-blue, hard and piercing, and yet intensely sensitive. Her mouth was set firmly; no smile broke upon it, and she said nothing. Only the rabbit moved, making its way off the girl's lap, hopping nimbly along the log, and then ambling over to Brendan where it proceeded to sniff the lower part of his legs. It rose on its hind paws and regarded him inquisitively, cocking its head slightly and pushing its ears forward. It rested its front paws briefly on Brendan's knee while it completed the inspection, and then made its way back to the apparent comfort of the girl's lap. She was still looking at him with the same impassive expression. The man was leaning towards him, his face wreathed in a benevolent smile.

No one spoke for a length of time that seemed interminable to Brendan's fevered mind. The man continued to smile, and the little girl continued to watch Brendan with an expression he found hard to interpret. It was neither friendly nor malevolent. There was no welcome in her granite eyes, only a quality of searching and assessment so incisive as to pierce him through the forehead and send a burning sensation seeping down to his gut. The rabbit dozed comfortably. The silence was broken when the man spoke again.

"It's your turn to open the conversation this time, Brendan. You have forty years of learning behind you. What do you have to say for yourself? And what would you like to know? You had plenty of questions as a child; you must have even more now."

Having been unprepared to become a part of some magical tableau, Brendan was equally unprepared to take the lead in whatever was being played out in it. His sense of unease was apparent as he asked

"So, are you the same man ...?"

"Man!" replied the stranger with mock gravity. "Man? You still think I'm a man? What do you see?"

"A farmer."

"And what did you see the last time?"

"A monk, or somebody who looked like a monk. Or the Devil. I thought you might be the Devil, or an angel."

"And what did I tell you?"

Brendan began to feel foolish. He felt cowed and on trial. He was a middle aged man, and one who had observed a good many sides of the human condition, but he felt like a child again. He was old enough not to hang his head in submission, and so he didn't. He regarded the stranger silently, trying to remember what he had been told that day, back in the mists of an eventful life. He looked at the girl whose stare remained unaltered, and at the rabbit carelessly snoozing on her lap. He remembered.

"You said you were a projection. I expected a monk, so that's what I saw."

"Right; and what would you expect to see at the top of a farmer's field? A farmer, perhaps? So, let's have some questions."

Brendan felt fractured. He was at a loss to know what to ask because he was at a loss to know what was happening. He decided to air his confusion openly.

"How can I ask questions? I don't know where I am. I don't know whether you're real or not. Is this a dream, a hallucination, or am I really sitting here? I've spent the last forty years thinking the other encounter was just some trick of the mind caused by illness. In fact, I'd all but forgotten about it. But here I am again, and I'm not ill. I remember painting a window frame this morning. Did I fall asleep in the chair and now I'm dreaming? What the hell is going on?"

The farmer sighed almost imperceptibly, but his expression was unchanged.

"Brendan, my boy. Remember what I told you about the nature of reality? Dreams, illusions, hallucinations; they're all just levels of the real and the unreal, depending on how you look at them. When everything that's illusion is removed, all that's left is consciousness; but that's a bit beyond you yet, so let's keep it simple. Yes, this is an illusion, but so is your life down there at the foot of the hill. So are your dreams; so are your imaginings. All unreal. And yet you have to treat them as real while you're a part of them. So trust your senses, old fellow. This is a real as anything else. You're in it, so live it. Of course, if you want me to, I could just send you to sleep. You'll wake up lying among the wild garlic surrounded by dark tree trunks, and you'll think this was just a dream. I could even arrange for you forget it altogether if that's what you'd like me to do. Then you can walk home and be none the wiser. Is that what you want, or would you prefer something a little more interesting, more adventurous? How would you like to take a journey with our young friend here?"

Brendan looked uncertainly at the girl again.

"A journey?"

"Yes, a journey. She wants you to help with something, and in the process of doing that she'll show you some pretty interesting stuff, I can assure you. You'll learn a lot, too. I told you that life was all about learning didn't I? I know you've already learned a lot, but it's been mostly – what should we say – academic. Now you get the chance to see some of it in action. You'll even come out of it still with a human body – that thing you're so attached to, the one you think is real."

The farmer's smile carried a hint of mockery, but it was gentle and benevolent. Brendan felt more nonplussed than ever. Being there at all was difficult to grasp; being informed that it was only the beginning of an unimaginable opportunity stood at the limit of his comprehension. The prospect of adventure had always appealed to him, but his first instinct was caution.

"Who is she?" asked Brendan.

The farmer looked askance for a second, and stole a smirk at the girl.

"Shall I tell him?" he asked her playfully.

The girl was stroking the rabbit fondly between its ears, but her stare remained as hard as ever. Brendan took a moment to regard her more closely. She looked to be around nine or ten years old, her skinny frame having the look of a waif, and her jet black hair tumbling untidily either side of her narrow shoulders. Her simple, sleeveless dress hung loosely about her insubstantial frame and finished just below her knees. Her little legs culminated in tiny, unshod feet. The dress itself had a sheen so lustrous that the apparently printed pattern was difficult to make out, but it seemed to be an interweaving of green leaves and golden ears of corn.

"No," she said without averting her eyes. "It isn't necessary."

Her voice had the high tone of a child's, but there was a rough, gravely quality about it; and even those few brief words carried the unmistakeable hint of an Irish accent. And then she addressed Brendan directly.

"So, do you want to come with me or not? No conditions."

Brendan looked back at the man, questioning him silently with his eyes. He had no doubt that the enigmatic stranger, who could seemingly appear in whatever guise he wished, was in charge of proceedings. He hoped for more information.

"Straight question, Brendan. A straight 'yes' or 'no' will do."

Brendan felt exasperated enough to splutter a weak protest.

"How can I say yes or no? I don't know who you are; I don't know who she is; I don't know where she wants to take me; and I still don't understand what the hell I'm doing here. No, let's make it more simple. I still don't know where 'here' is."

His two companions looked at each other briefly, and then looked back at him.

"All right," said the man. "I'll start you off with a couple of facts. One day you'll come to understand that you need to give up knowledge in order to gain true knowing, but for the time being I understand that the world you live in guards the pragmatic principle jealously, and that you are still in thrall to that principle.

"Firstly, I'm not anybody, at least not in a way you'd understand. I explained to you before that I have no body. As I said, what you see is your own projection which I simply enable you to perceive. You, on the other hand, do have a form of individual existence, as does our young friend here. She exists on a higher level than you, but at least you have that much in common. As for where 'here' is, it's simply one of those countless versions of reality I told you about all those years ago. I know you understand that much because I've been keeping an eye on your reading matter and the people you've been coming into contact with.

"You do realise, I hope, that you are more than a little privileged in being invited to undertake a journey that will take you beyond the world in which you're normally trapped. There are people who study hard for many years to be able to do something that's being handed to you on a plate. Not that you need be swayed by that, of course; it's your life and your choice."

Brendan realised that he did understand, but it was still a shock to find himself in a situation previously confined to book-laden theory, speculation and esoteric belief. How could he be expected to undertake such a journey? The landscape was unknown, the rules were unknown - even the very notion of reality was unfamiliar. If he'd been given a rowing boat and invited to make his way alone up the Amazon, he would at least have had some idea of what he was letting himself in for. But this? One phrase that the man had used, however, filled his mind and intrigued him:

"She exists on a higher level than you..."

There was something intensely thrilling in those few words. He judged that whoever or whatever the man was, one thing was clear: he was omniscient. And he could be trusted; of that he was certain too. Brendan's mind was already made up, it was just a matter of stating his decision. That was more difficult. He looked at the child again.

"Will *you* tell me who you are?"

He felt a sudden rush of concern. Did he have a right to ask her that; or at least, would her elevated status bring some form of indignant reproof winging his way? He didn't know who she was, but the man's earlier greeting had brought Titania into his mind. Goddesses are not always benevolent, and he felt he should exercise caution until he was surer of his position. There was no visible reaction in the child's demeanour, but the brevity of her reply was unnerving.

"No."

The farmer looked from one to the other and seemed amused. His gaze rested on Brendan.

"Well?"

Brendan's mind fell into turmoil again; but two strong, undeniable threads ran through the fog of indecision: the sureness that it would be unthinkable to give up such an opportunity, and a heady thrill of excitement at the prospect. Outwardly, however, he persisted in a show of reluctance.

"I don't really have a choice, do I?"

"Come now, Brendan, of course you do. Positive thinking, old lad! Do you want to go or not? The decision must not only be firm, but firmly stated. So let's hear it. Yes or no?"

"Yes."

"Good; that's settled then."

Brendan looked at the girl, wondering how she had reacted to his decision. A hint of a smile had finally broken on her small mouth. If there was anything truly illusory here, that smile gave the truth of it; for the tiny gesture conveyed infinitely more than the simple reaction of a ten-year-old girl. A wave of intense awareness flooded through him, so strong as to be almost palpable. There was mystery and mysticism in her small form, but outwardly she looked the same.

"Thank you," she said simply, without any affectation of pleasure or relief.

"Should I know your name?" asked Brendan. "I take it you do have a name."

The girl's expression changed to one of mild disdain.

"I do. I have several. For now, you can call me Annie."

At the sound of the name the rabbit became active, climbing up onto Annie's shoulder and watching Brendan steadily. The girl brought her lips close to the animal's ears, and said in a high whisper

"This is Brendan. He's coming with us."

"Does the rabbit have a name?" asked Brendan

"No; she doesn't need one. She's a rabbit."

There was that disdainful look again, and Brendan felt suitably chastened. He looked back to the farmer in hope of moral support. The log was empty. Brendan looked round in surprise.

"Where's he gone?" he asked.

"Gone? He hasn't gone. He was never here. He doesn't exist, as you understand the term. He told you he was a projection, didn't he? You don't need him any more, so now he isn't here. Confused, aren't you?"

Brendan shrugged.

"Seems I get easily confused. I dare say there's plenty more of that to come. Is it OK to ask where we're going?"

"On a journey."

"Yes I know, but what I mean is, well... Oh, I don't know what I mean. This is a lot to take in, you know. At least explain this to me: the man said that you and I exist in – what should we call it – an objective sense. But it's pretty obvious that we belong in different worlds – forms of reality, or whatever. So am I right in assuming that I've come out of my world and into yours?"

"Yes."

"And it's your world we're going to be staying in?"

"Not entirely. My world and yours are very close together, for want of a better way of putting it. Although my home is here, I can exist easily in both. I come into your world quite a lot, though I'm only seen when I want to be, and that isn't very often. It's a mechanical, sceptical world that humans inhabit. The fabric is too dense. It used to be different when your kind were more in touch with their roots – what you call 'nature.' Think of me as a part of the natural order."

"So, are you nature spirit?"

The girl laughed. It was a most engaging, girlish giggle.

"A bit more than that, actually. It's complex. Nature isn't just a biological machine, you know. You've read enough myths, haven't you? You'll find out more as we go along."

"Another question, if I may."

The girl inclined her head slightly, indicating acquiescence.

"Why do you speak with an Irish accent?"

"Because I'm using language to speak to you – in this case, English. Every vocal language has accents. You can't speak it without using one or another. My home has its point of contact with your world in the south of Ireland. The myth makers portray me as Irish, so Irish is how I sound. It's as good an accent as any. I could speak Greek or Mandarin Chinese if you'd prefer, but then you wouldn't understand me, would you?"

"There's something else," said Brendan, wondering how far he was permitted to take the interrogation. "You look like a little girl, but you certainly don't talk like one."

"I appear to you in a way that I think is most appropriate for the circumstances. It's all to do with being untouchable – for now."

The two of them looked at one another for a while, the confused, questioning eyes of the man Brendan finding no way through the impregnable shield of the child Annie. Brendan's mind began to swim again, and he was the first to look away. As silence enclosed him, the full gravity of the experience began to affect his senses, spreading outwards from his midriff, climbing up his spine, and seeping like an electrical charge down both legs.

"Do you have any more questions?" asked Annie.

Brendan shook his head.

"Right, are you ready to begin?"

Brendan nodded.

"C'mon then. No point in staying in this 'enchanted glade' any longer. It's a silly phrase, anyway. Follow me."

"Which way are we going?" asked Brendan.

"North west, of course."

"And which way's that?"

The girl swung her puny arm out and pointed across the middle of the pool.

"That way."

"Oh, right. Into the water then, is it?"

Brendan was joking. He assumed they would walk around the pool.

"Yes, into the water."

"You're kidding!"

"No. Water is my natural habitat."

"Well it isn't mine!"

The rabbit jumped off Annie's shoulder and raced for the pool where the insects were still dancing and skating on the blue surface. It leapt headlong into the water and disappeared from view. Brendan was shocked, but the girl smiled.

"Brendan, do you think I'd watch you drown before we were two minutes into the journey? I'm not here to lure you to your death, you know. Are you going to trust me, or what?"

Again, Brendan realised he had no choice.

"I suppose so."

"C'mon then."

They walked to the pool and stopped. Annie turned towards Brendan, took hold of both his hands and pulled him gently downwards.

"Kneel down, Brendan."

Brendan was unaccustomed to taking orders from children, and felt irritated.

"Why?"

"Brendan, this is my world you're in at the moment. I know the rules and the mechanics. You don't. D'you think it might be a good idea if you learned to trust me? If I tell you to do something, there's obviously a reason. Can we have that understood once and for all?"

Brendan nodded and knelt down.

"Right, open your mouth and take a deep breath."

As soon as Brendan filled his lungs with air, Annie brought her lips close to his and blew into his mouth. The pressure in his chest eased. It felt as though some invisible force was supporting his lungs and rib cage, and his mind felt suddenly sharper too. Even the colours around him became brighter and more vivid. The urge to breathe out was brief. He didn't know what was happening, but he felt full of trust and acceptance. Annie's precocious demeanour fell away as she giggled and clapped her hands together.

"Good," she cried enthusiastically. "Well done Brendan. That will keep you going for as long as it takes. Now we can be on our way. Hold my hand and walk with me into the pool. You're in no danger; just relax and enjoy the view."

Brendan stood up, took Annie's hand, and walked with her into the water. Some old instincts were still strong, however. He braced himself against the prospect of becoming suddenly very cold, and he closed his eyes until he was sure he was fully submerged. One note of relief, at least, was served; the water felt delightfully warm.

Waterworld

Brendan was aware of waking up, and assumed he had lost consciousness. For how long he didn't know. He could hear a child's voice echoing in his head. The words were unclear at first, but he was sure the voice was Annie's. He heard his name being called as his senses cleared.

"Come back to me, Brendan. It's OK. You're doing fine,"

He opened his eyes and saw the little girl floating perfectly still in front of him. The water was clear and brightly lit, but her form looked slightly misty and luminescent. Her face was unchanged, but her clothing was different. The patterned, sleeveless attire of the waif had gone and been replaced by a voluminous gown of ever changing blues. The dress rippled constantly, and the ripples shifted through a kaleidoscope of shimmering hues from petrol blue, to royal blue, to sky blue, and then to the deepest navy. Occasionally a highlight of the most vivid turquoise would flash and be gone again. Annie's eyes were on a level with his and they were smiling a reassuring smile. Her hands were held demurely in front of her stomach, and her raven hair swayed almost imperceptibly in the still, warm water as bands of light and shade moved slowly back and forth.

He looked down and saw that he was standing on the bed of the pool. Copper coloured pebbles stretched as far as he could see, interspersed here and there by dark green stones with star shaped silver growths on them. A little way off he saw another forest, but this time the trees were the green stems of reeds, rising in legions and swaying slowly and in perfect ensemble like a chorus of graceful dancers. Large plants with fronds the colour of aubergine grew in gay abandon in several places. They swayed gently too, shamelessly caressing everything within their orbit, and fish of many vivid hues swam in and out of the reed jungle. Their colours startled him. He expected silver, as would be normal in a freshwater pool. Instead there were blues, purples, bright reds and pinks. Some had spots, some had stripes, and some had complex patterns that seemed to change as they swam. Far from being camouflaged against their environment, they stood out in individual splendour.

He looked up at the surface, trying to gauge how deep he was standing. It was impossible to tell. Somewhere high above was an unsteady ceiling illuminated by the bright light of what he assumed to be the sun. He realised that he could assume nothing here. This was a country more foreign than anything he had previously dreamt of. The dark silhouettes of water lilies congealed into a bank of solid substance just above his head. He remembered that water lilies should be green, with little jewels set in the centre. This is a world in reverse, he thought.

A brief sense of panic struck him. He was under water. He thought about his breath, and became aware that he was still holding it. And then he questioned the fact, because there was no effort involved. It seemed his breath was holding itself. He felt no urge to breathe, but that offered its own problem: if he couldn't breath, how could he talk to Annie? He looked back at her.

She was almost hidden from him now, surrounded by small forms flitting back and forth - swimming around her, touching her, and looking into her face. They were the size of children, apparently the same age as her, but their forms were indistinct. They all seemed to have the same long black hair, although he thought he could detect a hint of green now and then when the sunlight struck it. They appeared unclothed, but he couldn't tell; the bodies were silver and glowed slightly. Small flashes suggested the possibility of scales, but he couldn't be sure of that either. The only features he could see clearly were their eyes, and they were full of expression.

So were Annie's. It seemed she was communicating with them for the expressions changed constantly, indicating questions, concern, interest, and final understanding. They all turned as one and looked at him, their eyes growing wide with wonder. They left Annie and darted in his direction. They swam around him at lightning speed, stopping briefly to look at one part of him or another. One of them brought her face to within a few inches of his and he stared into her eyes. They were the darkest and most beautiful emerald he had ever seen. Their owner must have understood his reaction, for the eyes smiled shyly. He observed that they had the same Gaelic look as Annie's. And then the figures cleared the space between Annie and him, becoming even more indistinct as they retired a short distance away.

Annie moved effortlessly towards him and stretched out her hands. He took them in his own and heard her voice echoing in his head again.

"Welcome to my world, Brendan. Do you like it?"

Brendan was confused. How could he answer if he couldn't speak?

"You don't need to speak," she said immediately. "Just think your thoughts and I'll hear them. And just in case you're worried about your privacy, there's no need. I'll only hear what you want me to hear."

"It's a very beautiful place," he replied "like nothing I've ever seen. Who are those figures?"

"You might call them my sisters... my compatriots... my friends. Distinctions aren't so clearly drawn here."

"They seemed alarmed at my presence."

"They haven't seen a human down here before. I'm not in the habit of bringing your race into my world. I've had lots of dealings with them, but always in your world. Human men are no strangers to me, but most of my sisters have only ever watched them from a distance. They find humans threatening. They are water creatures, pure and simple. Their forays above the surface are made only out of natural inquisitiveness, whereas I have work to do on the land, in both my world and yours."

"What sort of work?"

"You'll find out in due course."

Brendan looked around again, marvelling at this liquid realm in which only the copper pebbles and the stones were still. The movement of some of the plants intrigued him. The reeds that had their heads above water would be blown by the wind, but what of those that were wholly submerged? There was no palpable flow of water in the pool, and he wondered whether the plants in this world might have the means to move on their own. Maybe they were even sentient. He decided to be careful where he trod. He stooped to pick up a pebble and was briefly surprised by the slowness of his movement. He grabbed a large one and, even in that buoyant medium, it felt much heavier than he'd expected.

"Can I take one of these?" he asked.

"Of course."

"What I mean is, will I be able to take it back to my world as a keepsake, or will it disappear?"

"No, it won't disappear. The occupants of this world often take things from yours, so why not take something in return? Nobody owns them. Nobody can own the things of nature; that's just a silly human conceit."

Brendan regarded its shiny form for a few seconds, and then placed it in his pocket.

"Are you ready to move on now?" she asked him.

"I suppose so. Where are we going?"

"Home."

"What, already?"

"Not your home, my home."

"Oh, right. And how far's that?"

"Not far. Distances are measured differently here. You don't have to walk, anyway. Hold my hand and we'll swim together."

Annie gripped Brendan's hand with her small fingers. He felt himself being lifted, and then they moved forward towards a gap in the reeds. They passed through swiftly and Brendan saw the bottom of the pool fall away with a steepness that he found briefly unnerving. Soon there was only endless water in all directions. He had an impression of being in the depths of a mighty ocean, but the rose glow that suffused it reminded him that this was no earthly sea. He turned his head as far as he was able, and saw the silver nymphs following. Six or seven pairs of dark green eyes stood out against their hazy forms as they maintained a steady distance a little way behind.

"Your sisters are coming, too," he said.

"They're concerned for my welfare."

"Why? I should think you could probably destroy me if you wanted to."

"Yes, I could, but it wouldn't be quite as easy as you suppose. I'm not omnipotent, you know; I'm a material being as you are. I have powers that you would think of as magical, but they do have limits."

She stopped suddenly and pulled Brendan around to face her. She held both his hands while a serious expression came over her face. Her eyes seemed to darken, and the freshness of their apparent youth gave way to a glint of the hardest diamond.

"I need to say something to you, Brendan. Try never to make me angry. I have emotions; I get angry sometimes; it's a part of what I am. I'm known among men for my anger, even though it usually cools as quickly as it flares. Not always, though. Sometimes it burns fiercely until I have gained satisfaction for a slight. I would find it hard to destroy you, but I could make your life uncomfortable in a great many ways. I have no reason or wish to do that, but try not to make me angry; and for my part I'll try always to remember that you're an invited guest and entitled to immunity. Now, don't be concerned. I'm sure we'll get along just fine."

The girlish glow returned to Annie's eyes, but Brendan felt chastened as they continued on through the seemingly endless, pink-tinged water. He had questions, many questions. He wondered how much he was entitled to ask, and whether he would get answers he could understand. The voice in his head was loud and clear.

"You can ask whatever you like. It will be up to me whether I answer or not, and up to your own intelligence whether you understand. You can trust me to tell you the truth in all things."

"I thought you would only hear what I wanted you to hear."

"You must have wanted me to hear it."

Brendan frowned. He supposed he probably had.

"OK, let me ask you this. Just out of curiosity, am I capable of hurting you?"

"Only emotionally; not in any other way. You can only touch me physically as long as I permit it. You can only see me as long as I permit it. Why do you ask? Do you want to hurt me?"

"No, of course not. I just like to know where I stand. I'm in awe of you; you must know that. Any human would be."

Annie smiled, but it was not the innocent, juvenile smile he had grown used to. It was the smile of an adult and experienced woman. Its undoubted sensuality startled him.

"The men, Brendan; the men are in awe of me, even when they don't know who I am."

It was clearly an unintentional aside, for Annie's smile and general demeanour slipped easily back to that of a child.

"What were we talking about?" she asked. "Oh, yes. For the present we're partners, Brendan; but you might as well accept that I'm a lot more powerful than you – at least, in most ways. I think there should be no more talk of hurting."

They continued in silence for a few minutes more, and then he saw the bed reappear and rise gently in front of them. Annie let go of his hand and he stood upright, looking around at the view that was similar to the other one but with some marked differences. The copper stones were there as smooth and shiny as before, as were the large green rocks. There were no reeds, though, nor any of the multi-coloured fish that had so fascinated him in the other place. Nothing moved here except the flashing forms of the nymphs as they darted behind Annie and watched him over her shoulders.

The bed continued for a few yards to a sheer rock face of brooding black basalt. He looked up and saw that it climbed vertically to the surface, and then continued above the water. It was an unfamiliar sight in this watery world, where moving colours seemed normal. There was something forbidding about its hardness and its dark inscrutability. The water was clear, and colder than before. There was no pink tinge, just the harshness imparted by the rays of a high sun shining through the blue surface. He looked at Annie with questioning eyes.

"The living things don't come here," she said. "They're frightened of this place. They know it forms a boundary, and they fear they could be pulled into a world where they might not survive."

"Is that why we're here?"

"Yes."

"We're going through into another world?"

"Yes."

"What kind of a world is it?"

Brendan felt reluctant. He had a vision of some deep place populated by dark, demonic monsters with brimstone breath. Annie giggled her childlike giggle again.

"Don't worry. The world we're going to will be quite familiar and comfortable. This is one of many places where I can pass from my home in my world to my home in yours. They're always in water."

"So are we going back into my world?"

"Yes, for a little while."

Brendan felt relieved, and curious to know where they were. And then he had a sudden thought. He had seen no sign of the rabbit on the journey.

"What happened to the rabbit?"

"She went on ahead of us. She's like that – always in a hurry to get to wherever she's going. She's waiting for us on the other side."

Brendan pointed to the surface.

"Up there?"

"No. Through there."

Brendan followed the girl's finger to a section of rock face that he hadn't noticed before. It was round, about six feet wide, and glowed the golden yellow of saffron. It was right in front of him and reflected his image clearly. He saw Annie's reflection come alongside his, followed by one of the silver nymphs. The voice in his head was edged with a slight hint of excitement.

"Are you ready? It won't hurt a bit."

Brendan felt doubtful. He was human, and assumed that anything reflective was likely to be made of glass or metal. The same voice reassured him.

"Or water."

They shot forward towards the disc, and Brendan closed his eyes anyway.

"That's it. We're though."

Brendan opened his eyes. The transition had been almost instantaneous. He looked round and saw only grey water, laden with tiny particles that swirled without apparent purpose. He looked in all directions. There was no rock face and no disc.

"Where's it gone?"

"It hasn't gone. You just can't see it at the moment. You'll see it again when we're ready to leave."

Annie floated ahead and Brendan walked sluggishly behind her, looking around at a more familiar scene. There were no copper pebbles or bright colours here. His feet stirred up wisps of dark mud as he walked, and what rocks and pebbles lay scattered about were coloured the browns, greys and blacks of a typical lake bed back home. A dull, brown-green tench swam lazily across his path, and a black-striped perch rose to the surface and grabbed a fly, before disappearing into the grey gloom again. Soon he saw a wall of mud rise up to his left, and then another one to his right. It seemed they were entering the mouth of a small river and he hoped they would soon climb out of the water. It would be nice to breathe fresh air again.

He looked up at the surface and saw the silhouette of a small bridge etched black against the bright sky, and crossing the river that was rapidly becoming narrower. It was becoming shallower too, and he felt excited that his head would soon rise into wholesome air. And then he felt something move beneath his feet.

He stepped aside and looked down. What appeared to be the top of a scaly head with hair like seaweed protruded above the mud. It was the size of a human head, and the hair washed from side to side in the current. It lifted further and Brendan felt a knot of fear as two round eyes glared up at him. Annie's calm voice reassured him swiftly.

"Don't be frightened, Brendan, He won't hurt you. He's a friend."

Her small figure alighted on the river bed next to the creature, and she touched its head affectionately. A massive cloud of dirty mud billowed up as something big emerged. The cloud obscured the view for a few seconds, and then cleared as the current carried it away. Brendan stood transfixed at the sight. Something like a huge fish, at least seven feet long, rested on the river bed. Its head was almost human in shape but there was no skin to be seen, only creamy white, shiny scales with streaks of pink that could have been exposed veins. The dark green, slimy hair billowed around the side of the creature's face and thick neck, and the nose was a mere stump with tiny, forward-facing nostrils. Its pectoral fins culminated in large webbed feet like those of a reptile, and two others stood out in front of its tail.

The nymph joined Annie in petting the huge animal, clearly offering greeting. Its eyes looked between the two of them, and then stared at Brendan again. They were sad, soulful eyes, and a wave of compassion replaced his earlier fear. He didn't know why; he'd never seen such a creature and knew nothing about it. But the look of longing and desolation in its doleful glare held him firm.

A second cloud of mud appeared close by and another figure rose out of it. This one was very different. Brendan beheld a beautiful young woman with golden hair that glinted where it was touched by the faint sunlight penetrating the water. She was wearing a long dress of apparently rough fabric. The only adornment was a belt around her waist, held closed by a pinned buckle. It reminded him of things he had seen in museums. She looked quizzically at him for a few seconds, apparently searching his face to identify the interloper in her world. Annie moved over to her and they exchanged a sisterly embrace. The young woman smiled briefly at Brendan, and then knelt beside the creature. Its eyes turned towards her and carried the same searching look. She shook her head, looked back at Brendan, and then they both sank back beneath the mud.

"Who, or what, were they?" he asked.

"They were of a race little seen by humans, even in the old time. They're never seen at all now. They live in a land far beneath the bed of the river. The one that looked to you like a giant fish was a male of the race. The woman was his mother, and a princess in her own land."

"His mother? How can that be? And how old are they?"

"He is many hundreds of years old. She is considerably older. I'll tell you their story when we're out in the open air. Are you ready to go and see the grass and the trees again?"

"Can't wait."

Annie took his hand and began to climb the steep slope with apparently practised ease. Brendan felt his foot sink into the soft embankment, but found himself borne upwards surely and strongly. Within seconds he was resting on the warm grass of the riverbank. The sun was hot, and his wet clothes began to steam almost immediately. Annie waved a hand and they were dry. He lay back and looked into an azure sky, replete with high, cotton wool clouds. He felt again the sensation of having walked into a work of art or a photograph, something long established and unchanging, something familiar and reliable. The paradox of the magical and the mundane came with it. Confusion followed, but it was a careless confusion; it didn't threaten. He realised that this place was so essentially different from the glade; it was reassuringly mundane. And then a sense of the infinite came with his contemplation of the blue sky between the white clouds. He was becoming quietly lost in the concept of infinity, when the rabbit ambled up and nuzzled its nose against his cheek.

"Hello, little friend," Brendan said quietly. "It's very nice to see you again. We made it."

The Orphan

Brendan shaded his eyes against the sun and turned his head to look at Annie, sitting a few feet away and apparently enjoying the view. She was wearing the green and yellow patterned dress again.

"How do you manage to change your dress so mysteriously?" he asked.

"I don't. I don't wear anything. What need do I have of clothes? I appear to people in whatever guise I think most suited to the circumstances."

"Even me?"

"Especially you."

She continued to take in the broad panorama, and Brendan decided to do the same. To his left lay the small river out of which they had climbed. It was little more than a deep stream that had seemingly been waylaid before it had been able to grow into adulthood. A simple wooden footbridge crossed it a few yards further upstream. The structure looked fairly modern, but the stone piles on which it stood looked very much older. Ahead of him stretched the placid water of a large lake. Low hills fringed the far side, falling to a gentle slope on the other three sides that surrounded them. The foreshore was sandy in parts, occasionally broken up by groups of large, dark rocks that stood resolutely between the land and the shallows, as if linking one world with another.

At the far end of the lake was a small wood, and he saw a larger one clothe the higher part of the shallow hill behind him. A narrow road ran down from the high land to his right, came close to the lake, and then turned upwards to climb the hill beside the trees. He saw that the river soon narrowed to a rocky stream further up the slope where it entered the wood. The remainder of the view comprised rich green grassland, dotted here and there with the white shapes of grazing sheep.

"Where are we?" he asked.

"In Ireland."

"The Ireland of my world?"

"Yes."

"Is this your home?"

"It's one of them. All the loughs in Ireland are my home, although the main one is in Limerick."

"So why are we here?"

"I wanted to come home for a while. I miss it when I'm away."

"But why this one, and not the one in Limerick?"

"Because I wanted you to meet the princess and her son. I hoped it might teach you something."

Brendan was intrigued. He turned onto his side to better see Annie who was sitting with her knees up and her arms clasped around her legs. The rabbit had gone back to her and was lying asleep, stretched over her shoulder. She continued by asking him "What would you say is the difference between a myth and a legend?"

Brendan pondered the question for a moment.

"Never really thought about it that much. I suppose a legend is a story that might be true, but has no direct evidence to substantiate it. Or it could be a story about an actual person or event, but which has been elaborated and romanticised in order to make it more powerful. A myth doesn't pretend to be true, but is a fiction invented back in the mists of time to explain the origin of something, or maybe teach some lesson of principle or philosophy."

He was proud of his quickly contrived definition. He thought it erudite, and even felt slightly smug. Annie looked unimpressed.

"Right then," she replied. "I'll tell you a myth, shall I? It's based right here and centres around that little footbridge. Are you ready for a sad story?"

She turned towards Brendan, took up a cross legged position and placed the still sleeping rabbit on the fabric stretched between her knees.

"The story comes from a time over a thousand years ago, when the provinces of Ireland were kingdoms in their own right.

"It tells of a wandering piper who strolled into a village one day and played his repertoire of tunes. He'd come from the east and was on his way to Connacht, where he'd heard that the king and the people were generous to itinerant musicians. In time-honoured tradition he was suitably recompensed with a hearty meal, and when he had eaten his fill he took his leave of the villagers and came across those low hills on the far side of the lake.

"The footpath brought him to this bridge, which he meant to cross and continue his journey westward along the road there. To his dismay, he found it guarded by a large and loathsome creature. It appeared to be half-human and half-fish, and roared frighteningly at him. It spoke sternly, issuing him with a challenge.

"He was invited to play a tune. If the fishman liked it he would be allowed to cross the bridge. If he didn't, the piper would be cursed and unable ever to play a note again. As an added incentive, the creature made him an offer.

"'If the tune is the best I have ever heard,' he said, 'I will make you a gift of the greatest value imaginable.'

"The piper considered his position and realised that he had three options. He could fight the creature for access to the bridge, he could turn around and go off in another direction, or he could accept the challenge.

"The first was summarily dismissed. He was a musician not a warrior, and the creature was bigger and more fearsome than any human he had ever seen. The second seemed the easiest option, but he couldn't be sure that the fishman wouldn't appear on any bridge that he tried to cross, and that he would have to accede to his wish sooner or later. The only course of action was to accept the challenge. Like most people who play music for a living, he had a high opinion of both his skill and the quality of his tunes, and believed he would have no trouble pleasing even the harshest of critics.

"He sat down on the grass and played the longest and best of the tunes in his repertoire. All the time he was playing, the fishman sat silent and impassive on the bridge, and remained in the same posture for some minutes after the piper had finished. Then he turned his face towards the anxious player and fixed him with a cold glare. The piper feared the worst, but the creature spoke quietly.

"'That was indeed the best music I have ever heard,' he said. 'You may cross the bridge if you want to. But first I will give you my gift.'

"The piper became drowsy and fell into a deep sleep. When he woke up he saw, sitting next to him, the fairest maiden he had ever seen in all his long travels. He sat up and looked around for the fierce creature that had been guarding the bridge. He was gone; the beautiful girl was his only companion and he asked her who she was.

"'I am the gift my father promised you. I am yours to wed and keep by you all your life. I will never grow old or less beautiful, and when you die I will return to my own people.'

"'But how can a maiden as beautiful as you be the daughter of such a hideous creature?' asked the piper.

"'All the females of my race are like me,' she replied. 'The males are like my father. We do not find them offensive because of their appearance, but judge them by their deeper qualities.'

"The piper felt ashamed of his hasty remark and apologised. His companion smiled her acceptance. He fell in love with her immediately and was beside himself with joy. He prepared to cross the bridge with his new companion, intending that they should marry when they arrived in Connacht. The maiden, however, held back.

"'There is one condition my father did not make clear to you,' she said. 'I am not permitted to leave this kingdom. We must make our home here. But I have magic enough to ensure that we shall never want for anything, and you can spend the rest of your days playing tunes and writing new ones.'

"The piper found the prospect of being free to continue playing his music, without the continual pressure of earning his next meal, appealing. Furthermore, he decided it was about time he settled down anyway. And so they walked back to the village and were married before the sun went down. One of the local farmers, knowing that the maiden was possessed of great magic and wanting to keep her favour, gave them one of his barns in which to make a home.

"The piper could ask for nothing more, except one thing; and that was soon to be granted. Before three full moons had passed, his wife became pregnant and he looked forward to making his new life complete by becoming a father.

"Every night through the harsh winter that followed, his wife would sit by the fireside with her hands resting on her burgeoning stomach and he would play his music to her.

"'Listen,' she would whisper to the tiny life growing inside. 'Listen to your father's beautiful music. It is how you will know him when you are born.'

"A year to the day since his encounter with the fishman, the piper's wife announced that the birth was imminent. It had been a blissful year, full of love and comfort and the promise of a golden future; and that future was about to be augmented with the arrival of his first child.

"He paced back and forth anxiously while the village midwife attended the delivery in a room above. After many hours of nervous anticipation he heard an unearthly, blood-chilling sound come from the upstairs room, followed by the alarmed shriek of a woman. The midwife ran downstairs and proceeded at full tilt out of the door. The piper ran in the opposite direction, and burst into the bedroom to find his wife cradling a tiny version of the creature that had been guarding the bridge.

"'It is a boy,' she said nervously.

"The piper stared at his son in shocked silence, and then stumbled back down the stairs and out of the house. He went straight to the village ale house and became very drunk. The local men looked away and spoke in whispers, for the midwife had already given them the news.

"From that day on he became morose and constantly angry. He refused to speak to his wife, except to complain about anything he could find to complain about, and would not even look at his son. No amount of crying and pleading by her made any difference. Eventually she could bear it no longer and told him that she had no option but to return to her own people.

"'Do what you want,' he said, 'as long as you take the creature with you.' And then he went out to get drunk again.

"He slept under a tree that night. When he returned home the next morning his wife and child were gone, and he knew that his hope for a golden future had gone with them. He packed his few belongings and set off at dusk to continue his old life. The following day his body was found floating in the lake below the bridge. Whether he had slipped in the dark, or had been attacked, no one knew.

"The maiden was never seen again, but the finding of the body aroused fear in the minds of the locals. Stories began to circulate, claiming that the making of any music near the old bridge – even the innocent whistling of a tune – was dangerous. It was said that a monster with the body of a fish, and a head that was half human and half reptile, would rise out of the water and attack them.

"Soon the tales gathered more detail. The monster was the son of the piper, they said, and he was searching for his lost father, knowing him by the music. That much was true, but then they became wildly exaggerated. They claimed that the child was seeking vengeance on the father who had disowned him, and that he dragged men to their deaths in the river below the bridge. That was untrue; the poor creature never attacked anybody.

"There was talk of laying a trap and killing it. The village headman was wise, however, and advised against it. He knew the power of the princess and her people, and so the matter was allowed to rest. The story of the lake monster became a taboo subject and passed first into legend, and then into the mists of mythology.

"To this day, though, it is said that a wailing can be heard on the night air whenever music is played in the local bar. It is dismissed as superstition, of course; it's just an old myth. Myths don't pretend to be true, do they Brendan? Any wailing is simply the cry of an animal or some strange acoustic effect. But there are still a few folk who will secretly advise the musicians not to play any impromptu music, should they have cause to go near the old footbridge across the river."

Brendan remained silent. He sat up, crossed his own legs, and regarded the scene in which the story was set. Annie turned away again, too, and looked across the lake. The rabbit woke up and ambled over to Brendan, leaping onto his lap and looking intently into his face. Brendan stroked her ears affectionately, pushing them gently back along her fur. The rabbit seemed content.

"She likes you," said Annie.

"I like her. I love animals."

"Why?"

"Oh, I don't know. I suppose it's because they have qualities humans don't have. They're uncomplicated and unpretentious. They show you just what they are – nothing more, nothing less. They don't have our hang ups and ego obsessions. They're capable of affection, bravery and even self-sacrifice when the occasion demands it. Does a dog care whether its human companion is handsome or ugly, rich or poor, smart or scruffy? No. Their expectations and attitudes are simple, practical and steady. They take what they need and don't brag about their achievements. And I'm convinced they're a lot more intelligent than we think they are."

He had been watching the rabbit snoozing in his lap, but then he turned to Annie who was smiling back at him.

"I don't even swat flies, you know," he continued. "I can suffer for hours even if I accidentally step on a beetle or a spider, and I try to rescue anything that's in trouble. I'm pretty hopeless really."

"Good," she said simply.

The sun was at their backs, and sinking lower in the sky. They sat in silence for a while until Annie spoke.

"It'll be dark in a couple of hours. We'd better start making our way to where we're going to spend the night."

"Where's that?"

"A cottage a few miles along the road."

"Why a cottage? I assumed you'd sleep out in the open. It will probably be a warm night. I'm sure I'll be OK."

"I don't need to sleep, but you're human. Not only do you need to sleep, you need to eat too, at least for the time being."

Brendan realised he was hungry. It was the first time he'd thought about it since he'd left his house earlier. The thought startled him. That walk up the hill opposite his house now seemed to belong to some other world, and to a time so far away as to seem unreal.

"But how are we going to..."

"Just wait and see," said Annie, cutting him off sharply. "The seeing is part of the learning. There's a time for questions and a time for seeing. Come on; we have a few miles to walk before it gets dark."

They stood up and Brendan stretched himself. He felt stiff. The rabbit raced to the bend in the road and then continued at full speed towards the wood higher up the slope.

"There she goes again," he said. "Off in a hurry as usual. How old is she?"

Annie looked at him with a hint of contrived, but tolerant, amusement.

"You'll be asking me how old I am next."

He thought it a perfectly natural question, although he had no doubt that the answer wouldn't be simple. He decided to leave that one for now. They moved off up the narrow road, Annie walking slightly ahead and Brendan following. The rabbit had disappeared into the wood.

Lessons

Brendan became aware of how tired he had become as they trudged up the long slope of the hill. The late afternoon sun echoed his growing weariness; it burned less fiercely now, and ragged ribbons of grey cloud hugged the horizon. The interweaving brush strokes of wistful white and glowering grey seemed like roughshod itinerants, disturbing the peace of the bright blue backdrop, and lent the western sky a wild and headstrong character that he'd always found seductive. The air was still warm, though, and he was sure there would be a fine sunset.

Annie was walking on the inside of the road, close to the grassy verge, and seemed determined to stay slightly ahead. He wondered why. There was no conversation as they climbed, but Brendan was content with that. He lacked the energy to quicken his pace or talk loudly. Fifteen minutes or so of walking saw them reach the corner of the wood, where its perimeter closed with the lane and then ran alongside it. Annie stopped and peered into the trees. Brendan assumed she was looking for the rabbit.

"Carry on to the end of the wood and wait for me there," she said. "I'll catch up with you. There's something I need to do."

Brendan couldn't be bothered to ask what. He watched Annie's small form trip lightly into the wood until she was lost to view among the trees. He trudged on, musing fondly on the prospect of supper and a peaceful sleep in a homely croft somewhere further along the road. He reached the end of the wood and sat on a stone to await Annie's return.

The sense of peace was serene, and powerful enough to insinuate itself into Brendan's lethargic mood. A gentle zephyr caressed the rough grass, and he heard the myriad songs of familiar birds filling the early evening air. No other sound disturbed the tranquil scene, and he turned his face towards the benevolent sun. This, he told himself, was the very definition of rest.

He had time to think now, and tried to run over the day's events in a mind that was becoming ever more resigned to the need of safe anchorage. The memories and impressions tumbled over each other, becoming jumbled and lost in a haze of untroubled bewilderment. He gave up the attempt and idly searched the view ahead. He had breached the top of the hill, and was now on the downward slope. The road was narrow - not quite wide enough for two vehicles to pass, he judged. It ran straight for some way, and then began to curve gently where it encountered the first outposts of another range of low hills a few miles in the distance. He squinted when he spotted a small patch of incongruous red, half hidden among the greens of the landscape. He hoped it would prove to be the roof of the cottage for which they were heading. He looked at the soft orange sun, now filtered by a light haze and sitting just above the horizon on the opposite side of the road. It looked weak and tired, but still proud, as it came close to completing another diurnal journey in the never ending cycle. Those grey daubs of cloud that came within the dying master's influence appeared even wilder, their tattered garb now decorated with flaming fringes of hot orange.

The day was nearly done, and Brendan hoped that Annie would soon appear with the errant rabbit and they could continue onwards to a much needed rest. He yawned long and wide, and then heard a rustling in the wood. He turned and saw Annie striding petulantly towards him. The rabbit was coming too, but seemed to be keeping a studied distance. Annie looked angry. As she came closer, Brendan was taken aback. Her face looked older, and the dress she was wearing was flickering, uncertainly it seemed, as though it were going through a process of re-asserting itself. The impression faded as she came to within a few yards of him and stopped. She was, to all appearances, the same little girl dressed in the same simple frock. Brendan wondered why she was standing there, apparently trying to compose herself.

"Is there something wrong?" he asked.

"He rejected me. He said he didn't believe I was real, that I was just a figment of his imagination. Imagination, indeed! I gave his third eye all the power it needed to see me, and he didn't believe it. This is intolerable. I won't be rejected. Such bare-faced impudence! He's going to suffer; I'll see to that."

Brendan was mystified. Many obvious questions ran through his mind, but he decided against asking them. Although Annie was now the same child he had travelled with, she had the look of someone who would not take kindly to being interrogated. He chose not to guess who the "he" was, or in what way he had rejected her. She stood and stared at the ground for a few moments more as the rabbit reached Brendan and sat by his leg, watching Annie with an evident hint of tension. The little girl became calmer and more composed. She looked briefly at Brendan with searching eyes, and then regarded the rabbit with a smile. The rabbit ran to her, leapt into her outstretched hands, and was rewarded with a loving cuddle.

"Come on," she said to Brendan. "Let's be making for the cottage. It's about time you had something to eat."

Brendan rose wearily to his feet, and then they strolled side by side towards the hills in the distance. Neither of them spoke for some minutes, until Brendan looked over to his left. He had been right about the sunset; it was glorious indeed, and he remarked on its beauty. Annie looked at him questioningly.

"So you think the sunset is beautiful?"

"Of course."

"Why?"

"Well... the vivid colours, the scale, the forms..."

"You think beauty is contained within the physical forms of things – a sunset, a rose, mist over the mountains maybe?"

"Things can be beautiful or ugly, yes. Why not?"

"Well, it depends on what level you look at them. The man who introduced us would tell you that all material is illusion. But even if you accept the reality of the physical, as those of us with physical forms have to do, the concept of beauty being contained within it is still flawed. Things you call 'beautiful' are simply combinations of form and colour. Why should some be beautiful and some not? Answer: because certain combinations trigger the perception of beauty that is already there; it's a part of your higher consciousness. The perception of beauty is one of the things that connect the human mind with the highest level of reality. You don't need to see things you call beautiful in order to appreciate beauty. You can learn to trigger that perception at will, if you really want to."

"How?"

"Ah, that's not for me to teach you. That lesson comes much further down the line, when you're preparing yourself to rise to higher levels. All I can do is help you with some basic facts."

The facts didn't sound so basic to Brendan. If this was basic, he wondered how much deeper the advanced stuff would be. He shook his head and shrugged.

"So I won't learn it on this journey?"

"No. For now, try to understand that the sunset is only real in a limited sense, but the beauty is truly real in the most meaningful way."

Brendan was tired; he decided he would have to sleep on that one and ponder it another time. The rabbit had already leapt out of Annie's arms and was scampering ahead. Before long they rounded a bend in the lane, and a large croft, painted white and with red tiled roofs, lay a short distance ahead. It had obviously been enlarged and renovated. A flat-roofed extension had been added at the back, and the outbuilding had been put to use as a garage and shed. A well tended garden comprising a lawn and herbaceous borders occupied the land at the front. It looked in fine order, and comfortable.

"Who lives here?" he asked.

"A young couple in their thirties. He's a teacher at the village school over the hill. She spends her time making craft items and selling them at fairs around the country. I've used them before. They're susceptible."

"Susceptible to what?"

"To my influence, what else?"

"Really? That sounds interesting. I'm going to see you work your magic with people now, am I?"

"Certainly not. You don't get to see my secrets that easily. Wait here."

Annie walked off with the rabbit at her heels and knocked firmly on the door of the croft. It opened and she stood talking quietly to the occupant for a few seconds. The door opened wider and she walked in, the rabbit following close behind. Shortly afterwards she came back out and beckoned Brendan. She waved him through the door and shut it behind them.

"Meet Mr and Mrs Rafferty," she said.

Mr and Mrs Rafferty were sitting together on the sofa in a square room full of modern furniture and fittings. They smiled at him, but didn't speak. The wall on one side had a door in the far corner, no doubt leading to the bedroom. The back wall had another door and an open serving hatch, through which he could see the kitchen. Brendan offered a few words of greeting and thanks for their hospitality. The couple continued to smile back benignly. Brendan had the impression they were in a mild form of trance.

"Sit here," Annie said to him, motioning him to an armchair. He did as he was instructed and looked between her and the Rafferty's while Annie occupied the chair opposite. She turned sideways to face their hosts, and pulled her feet onto the seat. The rabbit took up a position on her legs, also watching the couple. Mrs Rafferty seemed prodded into action by the double assault, and broke the brief silence.

"You'll be ready for your supper then, Brendan."

Brendan looked at her for a few seconds. She seemed almost to be reading from a script, and the curious nature of this surreal tableau had him slightly bemused. He glanced at Annie, who nodded.

"Er, yes. Yes, I suppose I am."

"I have some vegetable stew in the pan. We're vegetarian, you see. And soda bread. You like soda bread, I expect."

"Soda bread?" He stole a glance at Annie, wondering whether she could have had foreknowledge of his fondness for soda bread. She grinned at him. "Yes, thank you. I'm very partial to soda bread."

He watched as Mrs Rafferty rose and made her way to the kitchen. Mr Rafferty remained seated, apparently taking some curious interest in the pattern on the curtains. Brendan looked at Annie again, who lifted one eyebrow. And then he heard a voice in his head that clearly wasn't Annie's.

"She couldn't avoid that one, so you *did* get to see her working her magic with humans. If you think *that's* clever, wait till you see..."

"Shush," said Annie openly.

Brendan looked at the rabbit in astonishment; the rabbit was looking back at him. His mouth fell open as Annie continued.

"So you decided to talk to Brendan, did you? Just don't tell him any of my secrets, OK?"

Brendan pointed at the rabbit.

"You mean ..?"

"Yes, of course. She's very intelligent. She knows more about most things than you do. I just didn't know how long it would take her to trust you enough. I expect your speech about the animals did it."

Brendan's tired mind felt close to letting go, and Annie giggled again.

"Are you enjoying the journey so far?" she asked him.

He thought for a second, and then decided that any reply would be redundant. He sat back in the chair, looked at the unassuming Mr Rafferty again, shook his head, and then stared at the ceiling. And so they all sat in silence for about ten minutes, until Mrs Rafferty appeared from the kitchen bearing a tray which she placed on the table.

"You must eat this while it's hot, Brendan," she said in a familiar, motherly voice that seemed old for her years. "Come along; you need to keep your strength up, now."

Brendan wondered what Mrs Rafferty could possibly know about his needs or the state of his vigour. He glanced suspiciously at Annie, who continued to smile innocently. He heard the other voice, too, in his head.

"Go on, Bren. Tuck in."

He rose on tired legs to take his place at the table, passing the glassy eyed Mrs Rafferty on the way.

The stew was, indeed, very good, and he ate it in silence. Annie passed the time stroking the ears of the rabbit which was resting contentedly with closed eyes on her legs. The Rafferty's seemed content to sit together, smiling at nothing in particular and saying nothing at all. When he had finished, he rose to take the dishes to the kitchen. Mrs Rafferty spoke again.

"I'll wash the dishes later, Brendan. There's a date and walnut cake in a tin in the cupboard next to the cooker. Please help yourself to a piece."

Brendan liked date and walnut cake, and offered his enthusiastic thanks. He returned with a large slice on a small plate and sat in the armchair. He asked Annie

"Don't you ever eat?"

"Sometimes, just for the pleasure of it. I don't need to."

"What about the rabbit?"

Annie shook her head. Brendan finished the cake, and then addressed his hosts.

"Thank you again. I gather you're a teacher, Mr Rafferty."

"No point in talking to them," said Annie. "They'll only respond to me at the moment."

"Oh, right. So what do we do now?"

"For you it's sleep, I think. You must be ready for it."

The Rafferty's rose immediately, as though commanded.

"You can sleep on the sofa, here," said the woman. "Mr Rafferty will get you a pillow and a blanket. You'll be quite comfortable."

Mr Rafferty was already entering the bedroom, and soon returned with a thick woollen blanket and a down pillow. He placed them on the sofa.

"I think we should be off to bed, too," he said to his wife, who nodded.

All seemed ready for a peaceful night. It was several hours earlier than Brendan would normally have gone to bed, but it was at least dark outside and he assumed Annie would want to make an early start the next day.

The Rafferty's were just entering the bedroom when a frightful screech rent the air. It obviously came from outside, and shattered the peace of the quiet, isolated location. It startled Brendan, and he turned his head in the direction of the kitchen, assuming at first that it was the alarm call of a bird. He soon realised it was a different sound. It continued for much longer, and carried the impression of fear and pain, rather than warning. Whatever was making the noise, it was screaming.

"What the hell is that?" he asked, looking at the Rafferty's.

They looked suddenly more aware, and also confused. The looks they were giving him and the little girl carried a note of questioning. He suspected that Annie was losing her grip on them, and stole an urgent glance in her direction. She looked agitated. The rabbit looked worse; it was trembling violently, pushing its ears flat against its body and trying to burrow under Annie's arm.

"A rabbit," said Annie quietly. "A baby one."

Brendan looked back at Mr Rafferty, who was clearly still under Annie's influence because he didn't openly question the presence of strangers in his house. Instead, he told the brief story of how he had seen two tiny rabbits in the garden that evening. He said they must have wandered away from their family, because the nearest warren was in a wood some way further along the lane. They had run away at his approach, and one of them had taken refuge in the narrow space between the outbuildings and a low wall that ran the length of the property on that side. The poor creature must have been huddled in there ever since. That space was also a popular rat run, he said. The screaming continued, and Brendan felt the need to do something about it.

"Do you have a torch?" he asked.

Mr Rafferty didn't respond. Brendan looked at Annie, who pointed to a draw. Brendan collected the torch, and then dashed through the kitchen and opened the back door. He was facing the side of the shed, and saw something small come out of the gap and run along the back of the kitchen until it was out of sight. He shone the torch at the ground behind the shed and saw a long snout and a pair of steely eyes looking in the same direction. A full grown rat was apparently regarding its victim with interest. He walked quickly over to it, stamped his foot and shouted. The rat scurried away and Brendan shone the torch around the area behind the kitchen. There, pressed firmly against the corner of the wall, sat a tiny brown rabbit. It was no bigger than an adult rat and looked lost and frightened. It was staring at the torch beam, and Brendan wondered what to do. He realised that any approach might cause it to bolt, and the only place it had to go was back behind the shed. He decided to leave it be, but to keep an eye on it for a while.

He returned to the house and locked the door behind him. He looked through the window. Sufficient light spilled out to show the baby rabbit still cowering against the wall, seemingly paralysed by its experience. He watched it for a few minutes, ready to dash out again if it should come under attack. The poor creature looked so young, so helpless, so alone and afraid. Brendan felt severely distressed at its plight. He could see that it was trapped between the high walls; it had no means of escape from the horror which might still be lurking in the shadows.

Eventually he returned to the living room. Annie looked more composed now that the screaming had stopped, and had seemingly regained full control over Mr and Mrs Rafferty. They had gone, and the door to the bedroom was shut. He told Annie what he had seen.

"I'm not going to bed yet," he insisted. "Not for a couple of hours, anyway. I want to keep an eye on the baby – make sure it doesn't get attacked again."

Annie nodded but said nothing. She petted the rabbit that was now huddled under her chin and still trembling.

"That was horrible," he said. "Can't you do something?"

"No."

"Why not?"

"Because it isn't my place to interfere. I'll explain tomorrow when this is over and I'm feeling more myself. The suffering of animals affects me too, you know."

Brendan's nerves were on edge. He'd never realised how much a defenceless animal in that sort of peril could affect him. He was in constant fear of hearing that terrible, blood-chilling scream again. He hadn't even known that rabbits were capable of screaming.

Annie clearly wasn't in the mood for conversation, and seemed almost in a trance herself. He paced around for a while, and then found a newspaper which he tried to read sitting at the dining table. Every ten minutes or so he went into the kitchen and looked out of the window. The baby rabbit was still there, huddled into the same corner of the wall. His vigil continued for a couple of hours, and there was no further sound. At last he felt truly tired and in need of sleep. One final inspection showed the baby pressed tight into its meagre refuge, facing inwards with its eyes closed. Brendan felt that all he could do was hope. He returned to the living room, took his shoes off and covered himself with the blanket.

"Goodnight Brendan," said Annie with an untypical fondness in her voice. "I hope it will be a peaceful one."

Brendan closed his eyes and drifted quickly into oblivion.

He woke with a start, and saw daylight beyond the curtains. Annie's chair was empty. He went through into the kitchen and found her sitting cross-legged on the floor, with the rabbit in its accustomed place between her knees.

"The baby went back into the garden," she said. "There was no further attack. I didn't expect one. I hope it's gone home now. Get yourself some breakfast and we'll be on our way. It would be better if we were out before our hosts get up."

Brendan looked at the clock. It was 6 am. He toasted some bread and helped himself to the butter and jam that he found in the fridge.

"You won't need food soon," continued Annie. "I'm working on that one, but it's difficult in this world. It'll be easier in others."

"The kitchen looks pristine," he said. "Have you washed up?"

"In a manner of speaking. Let's just say everything is clean again. The Rafferty's won't know we were ever here. Get your shoes and coat on while you're eating. They get up at 6.30."

Brendan did as he was asked, and was ready to leave as he was finishing the last mouthful of toast. They left by the front door, now bathed in the low, early morning sun sitting just above the hill opposite. The air was crisp and clear as Annie shut the door quietly behind them. The smell of freshness instilled into Brendan a feeling of wholesomeness and optimism. He looked at the dew on the lawn, and his spirits dropped again.

"Oh, no," he said weakly.

A tiny rabbit was hopping slowly across the lawn close to the shed. Annie saw it too, and muttered

"I hoped his mother would have fetched him at dawn and taken him back to the warren."

Annie's rabbit was watching too, looking at the baby with intense interest. Her attention shifted sharply to a dense patch of flowers in the herbaceous border. She began to tremble again, and the air was suddenly filled with the familiar, agonised scream coming from the undergrowth. The baby on the lawn moved immediately, trying to bury its tiny form behind a large flower pot close to the shed wall. Brendan saw a movement in the undergrowth and hurried across to it. He saw a second baby, struggling to free itself from the jaws of a large rat clasped across its back. As Brendan got close, the rat let go and scurried away. The baby crawled out slowly into the open, dragging itself with its front paws while its rear legs trailed along the ground. It was still crying. Brendan looked helplessly at Annie.

"What the hell can we do?" he asked.

"Pick them both up and take them to the warren. They'll let you. At least I can see to that."

"But suppose this one's paralysed from the bite on its spine?"

"It might not be. Rabbits can sometimes suffer paralysis purely out fear. Of course, you can kill it if you want to."

Brendan had always had a horror of killing anything, although he done it occasionally with animals that had been clearly beyond saving. He decided to do what Annie instructed. He picked up the one on the lawn first. It fitted easily into his coat pocket. It cried while he was doing it, whether out of pain or fear he didn't know. Then he picked up the one hiding behind the plant pot. It offered no sound or resistance, and was placed in the other pocket. And then he headed up the road with Annie's rabbit close at his heels.

The wood was only a few hundred yards away. Neither of the babies had struggled during the short walk, and Brendan placed them gently on the ground. The paralysed one dragged itself forward as before; the other one sat still and looked around. He heard a voice in his head.

"The adults won't come out while you're here."

Annie's rabbit was looking up at him. He wished them well, and then walked back to the cottage where Annie was waiting.

"Find it OK? Good. Let's be off then."

They began to walk back towards the lake, and Brendan asked the question again. He had been horrified by the experience of the baby rabbits and wanted to know why Annie couldn't intervene.

"Why do you think? I'm a part of nature's mechanism, Brendan. I can facilitate certain things in certain ways, the ones I'm supposed to; but I can't interfere with the overall working. The rats were defending their territory. It's what they're conditioned to do."

"It's the one thing I find difficult about nature," said Brendan. "It can be so cruel at times."

"Not cruel, merely dispassionate. Nature has no conscience or emotion. She simply drives the material function. Nature is the true mother of your human identity, and so she deserves your respect, but she has no feeling for her children. She demonstrates the connectedness of things, but she also shows why material reality can never be perfect. It can be a lot better than this, as you'll find out later, but real perfection only exists beyond the material."

"So, if you're part of nature's mechanism, why did you feel distress at the rabbit's plight? It was obvious you did."

"Because the higher mind is in me, too. It's what you and I have in common. We both have the potential to transcend nature when we're ready."

Brendan was quiet for a while, but the screams of the rabbits continued to haunt him.

"I hate bloody rats," he said suddenly. "Nasty little creatures!"

Annie laughed at his outburst.

"I thought you said you loved animals. There's only one kind of love worthy of the name, you know, and that's the unconditional kind. You can't choose which ones to love and which not, just because they do things that upset you. If you're going to love animals, you have to love all of them. You can't blame them for not having compassion and behaving in a kindly manner to each other. They do what they do; it's part of the simplicity that you say you admire."

They walked on in silence for several minutes. Brendan had been deeply affected by the experience, and was fighting a troubled mind that kept wanting to fill his reluctant imagination with the sights and sounds of the baby rabbits' ordeal. He pushed them away eventually, and had a sudden thought.

"Shouldn't we have paid the Rafferty's for their hospitality in some way? Surely it isn't right to just use people without giving something in return?"

"I did pay them. They've been trying to have a baby for the past five years. Last night, Mrs Rafferty became pregnant."

Annie's face carried a radiant, satisfied smile. Brendan heard the now familiar voice in his head again.

"She's good at that. It's what she does best. And thanks for caring about the rabbits, Bren."

There was no further conversation until they reached the lake.

Little People

Brendan laughed as the rabbit rushed along a rock rising out of the lake, looked back at them briefly, and then dived headlong into the water.

"How does she always know where we're going?" he asked.

"She knows my mind as well as I know hers."

"So, who is she exactly? What I mean is, why do you have a rabbit as a companion?"

"She isn't just *a* rabbit, she's... how can I put it? Let's just say she's the mother of all rabbits."

"Oh, right. You mean she's the emanation of the feminine principle as it applies to the rabbit family – as it were?"

"My word, Brendan. That's impressive. Yes, that'll do."

"So why a rabbit? Why don't you have a dog or a bear, or something?"

"What animal is more renowned for its capacity for prolific breeding? Fecundity is my middle name, you know. It's largely what I'm about."

Brendan looked at the skinny little girl with the hard eyes, and wondered again why she appeared to him that way. He'd seen enough by now to be sure that the real Annie was something much more than what he was seeing. He wanted to ask the big question, but was struggling to know how to phrase it. She was looking back at him in a way that was friendly, yet somehow intimidating. It seemed to be telling him that now wasn't the time to be asking the big question.

He looked over the lake instead, and breathed in the soft morning air. A light breeze stirred the placid water, and away to his left the rays of the rising sun were breaking the surface into a gently undulating mirror replete with shifting, silver jewels. His gaze took in a wide arc, and he saw that the verdant landscape was at peace and preparing to welcome another new day. He squinted at the sun. It was strong again, and getting stronger. A profound awareness of the cyclic imperative came with it, and he felt briefly overwhelmed with a new understanding. The nature of that understanding was not clear yet, but he knew it had something to do with wholeness, with indivisibility, with connectedness, and the certainty of the inevitable. He was lost in mild reverie for a moment, and then felt Annie take hold of his hand.

"Good," she said quietly, sounding like a mother again. "Let it come in its own time. Never force the process of learning, Brendan. Somewhere deep inside you, you know all there is to know. All knowledge is within you, as it is in everybody, but you must allow it to reveal itself when the time is right. If you force it, you'll just become confused. I believe the expression you have in your world is 'go with the flow.' Just be, and let the insights take root when they present themselves."

Brendan felt emotional. Something of great import was changing the nature of his understanding. It came suddenly, and it was big; he knew that. It would probably take a long time to sink in; he knew that, too. Or did he? A second wave of understanding washed over him even more powerfully. He knew nothing. Knowing the fundamental truth of things was the end of the line, and only the unfathomable paradox of blissful oblivion lay beyond it. He wasn't there yet; the end of the line might be a million years away, or it might fall upon him tomorrow. He caught his breath and felt light headed; and then the moment passed. The world was just the world again, and his life seemed still to have a future. Annie squeezed his hand tightly and said

"Time to take another lungful of magic."

He was about to kneel when something caught his eye. A vague, unidentifiable shape was bounding towards them from the direction of the lake. It was hazy at first, but soon became a grey, almost transparent facsimile of the rabbit. It stopped when it reached Annie. He had become used to seeing strange things, and simply pointed.

"What's that?"

"What does it look like?"

"The rabbit."

"And so it is!"

Annie's tone was almost gleeful

"I think you should close your mouth," she said playfully. "The flies are gathering. Don't worry; it'll all become clear shortly. Are you ready to get wet again?"

Brendan knelt down, took a deep breath, and soon had his lungs filled with Annie's elixir.

"Come on," she said. "I'll race you to the lake."

She moved at lightning speed and won easily, finally launching herself from the rock with the grace of a bird and plunging headlong and almost silently into the water. Brendan jumped in feet first. Annie was waiting for him with her hand outstretched. She seemed impatient. She grabbed his hand and they sped towards the same rock face that they had come through the previous day. The golden hole was there, too, and Brendan decided to keep his eyes open this time. He wanted to know what passing through it looked like. It didn't look like anything; it simply went dark, and stayed dark.

He felt uncomfortable, but was reassured by the grip of Annie's unseen hand. He heard her voice as clearly as before.

"Don't worry; you haven't gone blind. You'll feel the ground under your feet in a moment. Just walk normally. I won't let you fall."

Brendan almost stumbled as his foot sank into mud, and then he felt lifted again until he settled on something hard like rock. He felt the breeze on his wet skin, and knew he was out on dry land. He walked forward into the intense darkness, and soon the ground felt softer.

"Kneel down."

He did as he was told, and felt tiny fingers massaging the centre of his forehead. The darkness began to lift and he saw Annie's face becoming clearer. Within a minute or two the daylight was fully restored. Annie was smiling and the rabbit was sitting in its accustomed position on her shoulder, watching him. She appeared normal again, and he looked around. They were in the same place they had just left, and yet it looked different. Everything of nature's construction was in the same place – the trees, the rocks, the lakes and the hills. But they were brighter and more richly coloured, and radiated a faint glow of their own. There were flowers he'd never seen before. The verges were carpeted with golden, star shaped blooms; and further up the slope he could see patches of blue, violet and red. This was beyond his imagination; he felt dazed and revelled in the richness of it all.

There was something odd about the road, though. It looked rougher, somehow, and shimmered slightly. He walked over to it and peered closely. What he was looking at was the earth beneath the surface, dotted with pebbles. The shimmer was the tarmac surface, rendered pale and transparent, as the rabbit had. He looked back at Annie, questioning her with his eyes.

"We're in my world now. It's the same place; we just crossed dimensions. It's very close to the human world, and anything made there appears here, but the substance is different. Things that are native to this world vibrate on a different wavelength to things that aren't. Wait till you see the cottage we stayed in last night."

"What about the people and the animals in the human world?"

"Yes, they appear too, but they look like rabbit did to you when you saw her come out of the lake. The only reason you could see her at all was because she'd taken the trouble to attune you to her energies. As I said, she likes you. I had to attune you to the rest. Close your eyes."

Brendan did so, and was amazed that he could still see everything clearly.

"You're not seeing all this through your normal eyes, but through the third one that's buried deep and needed switching on. You can breathe normally now, by the way. The air's perfectly wholesome."

Brendan let his breath out, and then breathed in again. Yet another delight assailed his senses: a sweet smell like wild honeysuckle filled him with a sense of calm and contentment. He looked at Annie who seemed to be in a state of deep trance. Her eyes flickered open and she held out her hand.

"Eat this," she said, handing him something that looked like a small piece of grey dough.

"What is it?"

"You wouldn't understand. Just eat it. It will avoid the need of food for the duration of the journey."

"Magic grub, eh?"

Annie and rabbit exchanged glances. Brendan ate the doughy substance.

"It doesn't taste of anything."

"No. Now eat this one," she said, handing him another ball from her other hand.

"What does that do?"

"It works on your body's temperature control system, so you'll be comfortable no matter where we are. They should both last as long as they need to. Are you ready to move on?"

They set off up the grassy slope, and Brendan wondered what would happen when he placed his foot on the surface of the road. He found himself standing on top of the ghostly, grey layer. He expected it to be slippery, but it wasn't; it felt like a perfectly solid road. As they began to walk, he looked at Annie's feet. They were sinking in and pushing the surface aside, like some transparent, viscous liquid. She saw his brow furrow and explained.

"Your sight is now attuned to this dimension, but your body is still human. Rabbit and I can change our vibrations to suit whatever dimension we're in. That's why she's walking on the grass. She doesn't much care for the sinking effect."

"I don't suppose it's possible for me to change my vibrations, is it?"

"It is, yes, but it would take a lot of training and practice. I could change them for you quite easily, and will later on when I think it necessary. For this part of the trip, though, I thought you might find it interesting to keep your human body."

Brendan jumped up and down playfully a few times, stamping his feet and revelling in the new experience. Rabbit jumped up and down, too, and seemed to smile at him. Annie shook her head disdainfully, and walked on. Brendan caught up with her and asked the obvious question.

"Are there people here?"

"Yes, of course, but they're a bit different from what you call people. I believe you met some once, back in that wood when you were a child."

"What, the fairies?"

"That's a word that covers a multitude of different beings from different dimensions. The Irish are a bit more sophisticated about that sort of thing. They recognise that there are different types of little people. Leprechauns are the best known example, but there are others. Where you come from, you lump the lot together and regard them all as childish fantasy. There are several of them watching us at the moment. They're confused."

Brendan glanced around excitedly, but failed to spot any small faces framed with dark, curly locks.

"Why are they confused?" he asked.

"Because they're used to seeing humans going about their affairs without being conscious of the little people's presence. Humans appear to them as giant, wraith-like beings - grey and transparent. That's how you appear to them at the moment. But you're obviously with Rabbit and me. They're used to us and we appear normal to them. They don't understand what we're doing together. I'll give them a chance to settle down before I introduce you."

They walked on for a while, and then Annie stopped and restrained Brendan. She seemed to be listening intently to something.

"Mr Rafferty is just leaving for work," she said. "You're going to find this interesting. Better stand on the verge."

A minute or so later, Brendan saw a car approaching. It was hazy and transparent like the road surface. He recognised the ghostly driver as Mr Rafferty, who waved to him. Brendan waved back.

"He can see me?"

"Yes. I've told you, you're still human. His car could still run you over, as well. He can't see what you can see, of course. He can't see me or Rabbit, or the two people watching us from that little knoll up there."

Brendan followed the line of Annie's finger and saw two small heads peering over the grassy embankment. They looked like children with long dark hair and pale faces. He remembered seeing them before, in the wood all those years ago. Only the hair was different. He smiled and waved at them, but they dipped out of sight.

"Let's go and see the cottage," said Annie, "and then we'll make the acquaintance of the little people."

Predictably, the cottage looked the same as Mr Rafferty's car. He could see features inside the house almost as clearly as he could see the ghostly walls, door and window frame; he could even see the low wall behind the property where the baby rabbit had cowered. He shuddered at the memory. He turned his attention to the sheds, and saw the wraith-like Mrs Rafferty sitting on a stool and working on what looked like an item of jewellery. He decided he would like to come back here one day when this adventure was all over, and make the acquaintance of the Rafferty's more conventionally. A tiny thrill touched his stomach as he thought he might even meet their baby.

"That's a nice thought, Brendan."

Brendan swung round and scowled.

"There; you're doing it again! You said you wouldn't hear what I was thinking unless I wanted you to."

"I didn't, not in any detail. The soft smile on your face carried some energy with it; I couldn't help getting the general drift."

"Mm... Remind me not to smile in future."

"I think it's a nice thought too, Bren. And I like it when you smile."

Brendan ran playfully at the rabbit, who scurried away and ran joyfully around the garden.

"We came here for a purpose," said Annie, tutting approvingly at the human and the rabbit playing games. "Go and feel the wall of the house."

Brendan did so. He could only just see the form of the bricks and mortar, but he could feel the smoothness of one and the roughness of the other as well as if he's been touching the wall of his own house.

"Feels solid," he said.

"It is solid – to you. The little people walk through it with ease. They can even walk through the humans if they want to, and sometimes do when they're feeling mischievous. You know that feeling you get when a sudden thrill passes through your body and you don't know why...?"

"So they can walk in and out of people's houses at will?"

"Here they can; their vibrational rates are very different from the human world. That isn't the case everywhere. In some dimensions the rates are similar, and your solid objects are solid to them, too. And some little people can only enter a human abode if they're invited. It's a sort of unwritten law. Shall we go and meet some now?"

Brendan's reply was pre-empted by a familiar voice.

"Can I help you?"

Mrs Rafferty was standing outside the shed door with her hands on her hips and a frown on her face. Brendan mumbled an ineffectual apology. Mrs Rafferty continued.

"Who are you anyhow? And why would you be running around my lawn like a mad thing?"

"Er, no reason. I'm just a tourist...full of the joys of spring, I expect."

"The joys of spring, is it?"

Annie was laughing heartily, and Brendan found it quite impossible not to break into a childish smirk.

"So will you be moving on and taking the joys of spring somewhere else?"

"Yes, of course. Sorry."

"Hang on a minute. Don't I know you from somewhere? You wouldn't be one o' them men off the telly who plays tricks on people now, would you?"

"No, no, 'fraid not. I'll be on my way then. Sorry to have bothered you."

The frown on Mrs Rafferty's face became more intense as he turned to walk away down the path. Rabbit was hopping around and kicking her legs, such was her glee at Brendan's discomfort, and Annie was still laughing.

"Come on," she said, "let's see if the little people can offer a better welcome."

"Are they safe?"

"Only if I succeed in persuading them not to roast you on a spit and have you with a side salad for dinner. Of course they're safe. They're even vegetarian. They and the animals are one big happy family. Will that do? Come on."

They walked back down the road as far as the top corner of the wood. Annie led the way between the trees until they entered a clearing which reminded Brendan of the one in which he had first encountered Annie and the rabbit.

"Another enchanted glade," he muttered

The morning sun lit up the glowing trees on one side, and the star shaped yellow flowers grew in dense clumps around the edge. The space in the middle contained a broad ring of stones, and Annie entered it. She called out in a language unfamiliar to Brendan, and then repeated the call in the opposite direction. Her voice resonated back to them from all quarters, puncturing the otherwise perfect silence. A sudden rush of small bodies flowed out and formed a tight knot around her small form. They were even smaller than her, and she had to kneel to embrace as many of them as could get close.

For several minutes there was only excited chattering. Brendan didn't understand a word of what was being said, and was surprised that they were all children. They all had the same black hair and pale, pretty faces. The boys' hair fell as far as their shoulders; the girls' hung down their backs like fine-spun silk. In every other respect their looks were as individual as any group of children would be. They were thin, but didn't look undernourished. Their clothing was simple and made of a fabric that looked like brown hessian. The chattering stopped suddenly. Annie and one little girl, who was hanging onto her arm particularly tightly, turned to look at him. Annie whispered in her ear, and she walked towards him nervously.

"Hello," she said.

"You speak my language?"

"We learn it from the big people."

Her voice was higher than Annie's, but had the same gravely quality that hers had possessed when she'd first spoken to him. He realised that she'd lost it now. Annie's voice had become much more adult in tone, and he hadn't noticed the transition.

"Do you like the big people?" he asked.

"They're OK. They can't see us – well, most of them can't – so we have fun with them. We never hurt them, though."

"No, I'm sure you don't. Do you have names here?"

The child nodded.

"What's yours?"

The child told him, but it was unrecognisable. He decided it sounded like Serafina, so that would have to do.

"I'm Brendan, and I'm very pleased to meet you."

"Would you like to come into our circle?" she asked him, her big, blue, innocent eyes making the invitation impossible to resist, even if he'd wanted to.

"Yes, please."

She took him by the hand and led him forward to where a mass of anxious faces were watching with interest. They came close as he entered the circle, and a little boy gained the courage to speak.

"Not many big people can see us. Why can you?"

"Because Annie brought me here to meet you."

"Who?"

The children turned as one to look at Annie, who brought a finger up to her lips. They turned back to look at Brendan.

"Would you like to see us dance?" asked Serafina.

Brendan could think of nothing he'd rather do, and nodded. The crowd of children retired to one side of the circle, all except five of them who plucked instruments seemingly out of the air. Two had whistles, one a fiddle, a fourth held a bodhran, and the fifth child laboured uneasily with a long wind instrument that Brendan didn't recognise. He was intrigued by how they had acquired them, and asked Annie.

"They can teleport objects quite easily here," she said. "They sometimes do it with the humans' things, and then stand around giggling while some poor man is going frantic looking for his screwdriver or something. They often put it back later, and find it even funnier when the human finds it in a place he'd looked in several times. It's a bit mischievous, I suppose, but they never take anything valuable."

The three of them retired to a group of flat-topped rocks on the edge of the circle. Annie sat on one that gave a perfect view of the area between the band and the prospective dancers. She beckoned Brendan to sit beside her, and Rabbit leapt onto her knee before stretching out and resting across both their laps. Brendan's first thought was involuntary, and inappropriately human.

"I hope she hasn't got fleas."

"Brendan!"

Annie's admonishment was loudly whispered, but was no less vehement for the lack of volume.

"Sorry." Brendan's apology was immediate and genuine, but then he frowned and looked at Annie. "There; you're doing it again! You're reading my mind!"

"Shh..."

"Nice one, Bren." Rabbit's voice carried an unusually lugubrious tone. "'I hope she hasn't got fleas.' I like that."

"Sorry."

"That's OK. I'll forgive you. Fleas have a right to their life too, you know. Anyway, I'll shake 'em off in a minute. That's if I had any, which I don't..."

"Will the pair of you be quiet!"

The long instrument set up a deep drone, and then the rest of the musicians struck up a lively reel. A pair of children, one boy and one girl, left the assembled ranks and began to dance. Brendan recognised Serafina and the boy who had questioned him. They stepped and switched their way in perfect ensemble towards the middle of the circle, turned to face each other, and then turned again until they were dancing back to back. They moved apart and each danced around opposite sides of the circle, before coming together again and dancing back to the assembly.

Brendan's delight was unbounded. Irish music and Irish dancing had long been a favourite. It had the power to move his mood into a lively but contented state, and this was the best he had ever heard or seen.

"They're married," Annie said quietly to Brendan.

"Married?!"

"Yes. Why not? I'll tell you more later."

The pair danced back towards the centre of the circle, but this time they were followed and matched step-for-step by two lines. The first line consisted entirely of girls; the second comprised the boys. They kept formation until they reached the middle, and then broke in opposite directions. The girls kept their arms at their sides and formed a circle revolving one way around the central pair. The boys stretched out their arms, linked hands, and formed a circle turning the other way and outside the girls. Rabbit leapt to the ground in great excitement and began what appeared to be a dance of her own.

Brendan was enthralled, and became even more so when the circling dancers somehow contrived to pair up, one boy to one girl. Some remained in position, while others moved at varying speeds until they formed a triangle. The dancing continued with the original pair at the apex until the band sounded the final note. They turned together to face Brendan and Annie, and bowed. Brendan applauded loudly. The band bowed too, and he called out "Bravo" enthusiastically. Serafina walked over and asked him whether he'd liked it.

"It was absolutely wonderful," he said with honest enthusiasm. "Did you learn that from the big people?"

"We did not!" replied the little girl with a sweet look of indignation. "They learned it from us a long time ago, before they became wrinkled and lay still. The humans always do that. Will you grow wrinkled and lie still one day, and then disappear?"

"Yes, I'm sure I shall."

"Oh well," she said with a shrug of her shoulders, and then returned to the others in the circle.

The children showed no sign of fatigue, but settled on the grass inside the circle and talked quietly among themselves. Some of them delighted in petting Rabbit, who was moving among them.

"This is their parlez time," said Annie. "They make all their decisions in the circle. It has a benevolent power, you see, and helps them make good ones."

"Decisions about what?"

"About how to keep themselves amused and occupied."

"What about their parents? Where are they? And don't they have Elders, or something?"

"No, there are no Elders; and they have no parents, either. They were never born in the conventional sense. They've been on the earth since the earth began, long before I was born. I've always supposed they came from the stars, but even I don't know for certain. They came as children, and they remain children. They can get hurt, but any damage regenerates; and there is no death here. They live in a perpetual state of childhood. They play, sing, make music, have fun with the humans occasionally, and commune with nature."

"You said they get married."

"Well, they pair up and go through a ceremony. They stay together for so long, more as best friends really, and then change partners every so often. And, before you ask, there's no sex here. There wouldn't be any point, would there?"

"Doesn't it get boring for them?"

"Not at all. They're content and joyful because they don't know any other way to be. There's one major difference between humans and the fey. Humans have bodies that wear away, or can be damaged beyond repair so that they die anyway. When that happens, the essence that occupied the body moves onto another one. You're familiar with the cycle of life, death and rebirth; I know you are. Humans are the most privileged of life forms at this level because they can progress towards release. The problem that brings with it is that you're born with an inbuilt need to develop in some way, and the human race has forgotten just what it is they need to develop. You're so convinced that material reality is the only sort that you lock your aspirations into it. You seek wealth, power, influence, fame – all those fleeting things that can only last a short lifetime. You become worried, anxious and frightened when anything threatens that material life. You could have the same joy and contentment as the fey, if only you'd stop chasing things that don't matter; and you'd progress faster, too. Joy and contentment is the natural state of all sentient beings, but you insist on blocking it."

Brendan went silent for a while, musing on what Annie had told him, especially the last sentence. A Taoist had once told him the same thing once. He watched the children who were now playing a game, chasing each other in and out of the trees. He wondered where his enigmatic companion fitted into the picture. He looked into her face and she looked back, her young and yet so ancient eyes flooding him with a sense of infinite knowledge and unfathomable timelessness.

"I'll tell you more about me another time," she said. "I think we should be moving on. I have a job for you to do."

A job? That was a new departure. So far he had seen strange things and learned lessons, some of which had already been taking root. He wondered what sort of a job it would be, but had the sense not to ask. Whatever it was, he would have to do it anyway. No doubt he would learn more in the process, since that seemed to be the point of it all.

He saw Rabbit running towards them from the trees, chased by a group of laughing children. She allowed them to catch her when she reached the middle of the circle, before squirming out of their grasp and leading them on another merry chase around the perimeter. He wanted to stay longer; such innocent pleasure struck him as the stuff of life's true imperative. But he would have to move on. Wherever Annie wanted to take him was where he would have to go. Rabbit leapt into his lap and turned to face the children, who were now approaching as if in answer to a summons.

Annie spoke to them in the same unfamiliar tongue she had used earlier. Serafina stepped forward.

"Goodbye Brendan. It was very nice meeting you."

Brendan fell to his knees, embraced her and kissed her on the cheek.

"Goodbye Serafina. I hope to see you again some day."

He heard Rabbit's voice, coming from the side where she had slid off his lap.

"You will."

Each child approached him in turn. Every girl exchanged a hug and a kiss on the cheek. Every boy received a hug and a handshake. Brendan looked back once as they left the gathering, and returned their wave. Soon the three of them were back on the lane and walking towards the lake. The sun was low again. It seemed such a short time since they had entered the wood that morning.

"Time works differently here," said Annie. "You must know by now that time is an illusion too."

Brendan merely nodded, and asked

"Where are we off to next?"

"East across the sea, close to where I was born. You can sleep on the way."

They went through the familiar routine when they reached the lake, and then leapt in together. Rabbit had gone ahead as usual. The hole in the rock face was a brilliant electric blue this time.

"That's because we're heading for the sea," said Annie, whose robe was coloured an array of shifting greens. Go to sleep, Brendan; you'll need your strength tomorrow."

Brendan felt extremely tired, too tired even to ponder the ominous implication of Annie's final words before he fell into a peaceful slumber.

Rescue

He woke up gradually and with reluctance, warding off the fully wakened state by keeping his eyes firmly shut. Anxiety was clutching at the space under his ribs. His midriff ached, and the cold breath of solitude infused a mind that seemed suspended between invisible extremes. He felt the texture of water clinging to his face, as he expected, but then a question struggled through to a brain that was still befuddled. Why only his face? If they were racing through an ocean, there should be more. It was all too still, too clinging, and too dark.

    He tried to open his eyes and move his limbs, but his body failed to respond to his will. It felt trapped, held captive by some power that had no form. Confusion and anxiety welled up together and he gathered the strength to try again. He felt giddy and dysfunctional. The anxiety grew to a state of desperation, made all the stronger by a familiar sense of claustrophobia. He was a child again, wound up in the bed sheets and unable to access the light and free air beyond them; he was locked once more in that dark shed with no means of escape and the night coming on; he was confined in the straightjacket he had always feared so much. His beleaguered mind was nearing breaking point and about to force a helpless scream from his lips. And then his eyes flicked open. He was standing at the bottom of his garden, being gently wetted by a light drizzle.

    He looked around in disbelief. He was awake, of that there was no doubt. His mind was fully aware and regarding the impossible. More questions tumbled through it in a jumbled mass. Was his journey over already? Had Annie tired of him and returned him to his own world? Why? Had he failed to live up to expectation in some way? Or had the whole thing been a hallucination, a dream perhaps? Had he walked in his sleep and woken at the bottom of his garden in the bleak half light of a watery dawn? He looked down at his clothes. They were the same as he had been wearing when he walked up the hill to the copse. There was no sense here. He patted himself to be sure he was physical. But could he be sure? Nothing was certain any more.

He sensed that the daylight was not rising, but falling, and his house at the top of the garden was unlit. He walked up the path, fishing for the bunch of keys in their familiar pocket. He found them and tried to unlock the front door. The key went into the lock but wouldn't turn in either direction. He tried several times but the result was the same. He repeated the exercise at the back door. No joy there either.

Some inner voice urged him to abandon the attempt, and the same intelligence forced upon him the growing conviction that Annie, the rabbit and the journey were real, and that he must find some way of getting back to them. That view was reinforced when he returned the keys to his pocket; his fingers brushed the copper pebble he had placed there. But how could he return? Where were they? What was happening?

He walked back down the garden path and tried to apply the light of reason to a situation in which there appeared to be none. He looked around and realised that things were not as they should be. It was early August when he'd walked up the hill, but the garden had the look of October about it. The summer flowers were gone, their heads reduced to dark husks and their stems drooping into decay. The light seemed eerie in the gathering gloom of dusk. It had more of lurid luminescence than of honest light about it, and the garden looked brighter than the deep grey sky could seem to account for. It was an unwelcome brightness, a wrong, unnatural sort: unwholesome and disturbing. He began to believe that it was only there to enable him to be watched.

He looked southward to the river valley, where the view of trees, fields and hedgerows was washed into a range of depleting half tones. Nothing moved there; the familiar lights of traffic running along the road beyond the river were conspicuous by their absence. Neither was there any other sign of life; the specks of brightness that usually betrayed the location of the many scattered buildings were absent too. And there was no sign of moon or stars in the saturated gloom above his head. This was an abandoned place.

He reached the bottom of the garden and became aware of one or two small shapes falling around him. They were decaying leaves, and confirmed that he had somehow woken in an autumnal world. The rain had stopped but everything dripped mindlessly and mockingly. The still, misty air felt cool, and the occasional clatter of a dead leaf was the only sound breaking the mortified silence.

He looked along the empty lane. Big old trees rose majestically out of the hedgerows every twenty or thirty yards, their massive crowns shading the road to blackness where the lane bent out of sight, a little way down the hill. The silent lane receding into darkness became a grotto that held the unwelcome promise of some unimaginable mystery. The sight of it brought the grip of anxiety back to his stomach. It called to him too, silently, but no less powerfully for that. Its dark, damp inscrutability tugged at him, and he felt he had no choice but to obey. He looked back at his house. He wanted to go in and turn the lights on, kindle a fire, and rest in the security of familiar surroundings. There was no comfort to be found there. The house remained unlit and silent. It rejected him. There was only one way to go.

He began to walk towards the bend in the lane. He passed through the shadow of the first great sycamore in the hedgerow, and then back into the jaded light beyond. That was the last of it. From there the trees were more closely spaced, and their combined crowns denied the tarmac surface what little skylight there was left. He continued into the fast growing gloom that seemed to have a life of its own, so surely did it encircle him with malevolent intent. His pulse was racing, his fear growing, and yet he continued slowly on. The power that drew him was irresistible.

He stopped briefly when he heard a rustle in the ditch beside the road. He knew that rats ran along there sometimes, but the sound was much too heavy for a small rodent. His eyes were growing accustomed to the low light, and he could make out the difference in tone between the dark verge and the even darker channel. He saw no movement in either.

He walked on until he came to the gate that led into the field with the copse at its crown. It was open, and the invitation to walk through was so obvious as to be unquestioned. But question it he did. His fear was growing stronger, but the force that had pulled him there was growing stronger too. He looked reluctantly at the space beyond the gate. It was the darkest place of all. He had been in there many times; he had walked along it only two days ago, but in the bright light of day. He knew that the track leading from the gate rose steeply between two embankments crowned with hornbeam and hawthorn, before emerging on a level with the raised field. It was a sunken place that might conceal any number of unimaginable nightmares. He had no choice but to walk through, hurrying forward to try and reach the open field as quickly as possible.

He heard one of the trees shake, and felt a shower of water fall on him from its leaves. There was no wind, and so the movement was inexplicable. He looked up at the black tracery, only faintly silhouetted against the darkening sky. The forms of the leaves and branches were jumbled, some open and some dense. Anything crouching there would be impossible to see, but at least nothing moved.

And then he heard more rustling behind him and turned in fright. The gate was now some twenty or thirty yards away and hardly visible, but there was just sufficient light to see that it was shut. Who or what could have shut it? A notion of entrapment began to take hold. He could also make out a shape in front of it, something at least as long as the width of the gate, for it stretched from one side to the other. It moved slowly away into the blackness, and Brendan thought he saw two red specks at one end of the moving mass.

But then the worst of horrors broke upon his ears. A long, low growl fractured the almost palpable black space between them. His fear was coming close to terror, and the need to flee paramount. The unknown horror was behind him; the embankments on either side were steep and slippery. His only option was to make for the open field as quickly as possible. His spirits were buoyed slightly by some unfounded belief that the creature could only move slowly; and then were dashed again when he realised that there might be more of them. But where? In the trees? In the field? His sudden dire and debilitating sense of becoming corralled by an evil presence spurred him to the only course available. He forced his shaking legs to run as fast as they could up the remainder of the enclosed track until he reached the rough ground of the raised meadow.

He looked around immediately, and saw no movement for a few seconds. And then something black, and of indeterminate shape, appeared briefly and seemed to slither behind a knoll. He looked around and thought he saw several more shapes appear and disappear among the dark grass. Their numbers continued to increase and they were coming closer. Inevitably, his mind flashed back to the creature he had seen in the wood all those years ago. Were these the same? The stranger had said they couldn't harm him, but his body had been human then. He didn't know what it was now; and there was no omniscient stranger to reassure him. He was alone.

He looked up at the copse ahead of him, the place where all this had started. He was beginning to wish desperately that he had never accepted its invitation. Every part of his body was trembling; he felt cold, exhausted and terrified.

And then his disbelieving eyes caught the most wondrous and welcome sight. Standing in front of the copse was a small figure. It glowed yellow and green in the gloom, and beckoned him with both hands. The prospect of deliverance gripped him immediately. His impassioned call was half shouted and half cried, and seemed to echo back from the leaden sky.

"Annie!"

The figure disappeared into the mass of trees. Brendan made what haste he could on weak legs, stumbling twice when his foot caught a divot in the darkness. As his breath grew shorter his fear returned, and rose unerringly with it.

He could see more shapes to the right and the left, appearing and disappearing as though they had some means of burrowing into the ground and rising again as the whim took them. Some of them stayed visible long enough to show how big they were, and the two red specks he had seen by the gate were confirmed as the creatures' eyes – wild and pitiless, and watching him with predatory intent. What logic he could still call on was asking him only one question: why did they not attack?

He assumed they were herding him, driving him onwards to some horrible end. He questioned the wisdom of making for the copse, for that seemed to be what they wanted. But what choice did he have? He fell into a desperate, confused state of mind, and a second question came with it: where was Annie? More jumbled thoughts followed. Had the sight of her been real? Could it have been a hallucination born of terror? Could the creatures even have produced it somehow, through some mysterious means that only existed here? Was it part of their strategy? How could he know? He was alone in a world where nothing made sense and anything might be possible. And then he heard the voice.

"Come into the trees Brendan."

It was Annie's voice, but could he trust it? He heard it again.

"Follow my colour."

He felt sick. Hope and hopelessness wrestled for supremacy for a few seconds, and then a flash of calm clarity broke upon his battered senses. He could trust it. He didn't know why, but that didn't matter. It was like the moment when he knew that he could trust the stranger in the wood. His intuition had been right then, and it was right now.

He continued to the copse and felt no hesitation as he entered the trees. There, running before him and winding among the trees, lay a band of mist. It was coloured blue, and shimmered through every hue imaginable. He laughed crazily, and his breathing became ever more laboured as he followed the mist deep into the wood.

He hoped the creatures hadn't followed him in there, but the hope was misplaced. The sound of tearing twigs assailed his ears. He looked to either side and saw that his tormentors were now only yards away and keeping pace, watching him as before with those hellish gashes they had for eyes. The growling began again too, not from just one throat, but from several. The frailty of his human brain reasserted itself, and he questioned whether he had made a hideous mistake. No, surely not; the ribbon of blue mist was proof enough. He continued to follow it and almost immediately found himself stumbling into that same amphitheatre in which he had met the farmer and the little girl. The misty band ran right up to the same pool that had been the start of his journey, but there was no blue skylight reflected there. Its surface was black, broken here and there by dull grey reflections.

He stumbled towards it anyway. Even in that darkened state, it held the promise of safety if only he could reach it. The creatures were closing in now. Two of them were already crawling slowly around the pool, watching him. He saw more appear on the other side, their red eyes adding fearsome reflections to the meagre ones that were already there. On both sides of him the creatures came close, and he could smell the horrible stench that he remembered from his first encounter. He tried to gather courage by remembering how his hand had passed through the black mist of the creature's head. The memory was far from clear in a mind that was falling apart.

The pool was only a dozen yards away, and huge black things with vicious eyes and predators' teeth were lining the path formed by the mist. He stopped, his fractured mind wracked with indecision. The available options were racing back and forth in panic stricken confusion, colliding with each other and falling without resolution. Retreating, standing still, walking the path between that hideous guard of horror – all promised the same merciless, terrifying end in a maelstrom of teeth and scorching breath. He was about to sink to his knees and give in to the inevitable, when he heard Annie's voice again.

"No, Brendan. Trust me. Keep going. The pool is your way out."

Some small vestige of courage reanimated his trembling body. He walked slowly forward, and the creatures continued to watch him. It seemed to take an age to reach the water's edge, but reach it he did. And then all emotional sense drained away. No fear, no trepidation, no doubts. There was only one thing to do. He leapt into the pool and sank beneath the surface, letting his arms rise above his head to minimise resistance.

A hand took hold of his wrist. He felt himself being lifted upwards, and fell weakly onto soft ground. He opened his eyes, but the sudden glare was painful and he closed them again. He felt something soft, warm and furry nuzzle his nose. He eased his eyes open slowly, and saw Rabbit looking at him with apparent anxiety. She burrowed into the curve of his neck, and then forced her way under his cheek to provide a pillow. Annie was reclining easily on the grass, displaying no evident concern. Her voice was calm and soothing, and accompanied by the lightest of encouraging smiles.

"Hello, Brendan. You're back with us now; it's all over. You'll be right as ninepence in no time."

The Execution

It didn't take long for Brendan's unbridled relief to turn to curiosity. He sat up and turned to Annie.

"Come on; enlighten me. Where the hell have I just been? What happened? Was it just a bad dream, or what?"

"Something like that. It was similar to a dream in that it was only your consciousness down there. Your body stayed with me."

"But I could feel the rain, I could see my clothes, I even felt the pebble in my pocket. Just projections, I suppose?"

"Of course."

"I was never in any danger, then?"

"Oh yes, you were in danger all right. Not physically, of course. Those creatures couldn't have touched you, but they could have seriously messed up your mind. That's why I had to get you back without too much delay."

"So the creatures were real?"

"Of course, insofar as anything is. You really should be learning that one by now."

"But, hang on. If only my consciousness was down there, how could they see me?"

"Those creatures live in perpetual darkness. Seeing in visual terms would be of little value to them. Those slits that look like eyes are actually sense organs, and what they sense is energy. They sensed yours and they were curious, especially since you were terrified and fear attracts them. They're attracted to all negative energies. If you hadn't got out when you did, they would have become ever more curious. They would have crawled all over you; they would have suffocated your mind. It would have felt lake having your body suddenly filled with writhing reptiles. I doubt you would have kept your sanity. No harm done, though; I got you back."

Brendan was horrified, and tried no to dwell on what it would feel like to be full of writhing reptiles.

"But how did I get there?" he asked. "Is it likely to happen again?"

"No. It was the time shift that did it. We were just passing what you call the Isle of Man. That's where I was born, so it's the most natural place for me to move into another time. When we did that, the shock sent your consciousness tumbling off on its own. You weren't ready for it, you see. That was my fault. I'll prepare you next time. Your mind tried to go home, to familiar and comfortable surroundings, but it got lost. It found the place you know as home, but at a point a little way into your future. That's why there was nobody else around; the other people who live there simply haven't arrived at that point yet. The fixtures are fixed, of course. What made it really bad was the fact that the part of your mind you were accessing was a very deep part, one you would never normally use. It's capable of perceiving a very dense level of reality – the one on which those demons live. You didn't know what was happening, so you didn't know the way out. Are you getting all this?"

"Some of it..."

"Oh well, you'll work it out eventually. I knew what had happened and was watching you all the way. The problem was that the vibrations down there were too dense for me to access physically. I tried to appear to you, but couldn't get down that low. All I could do was influence your mind. That was why you were drawn to the route you took. I needed to get you back to the pool, since I knew that the water would realign your mind to my direct influence and help me pull it back. I work well in water. Simple, really."

"But I saw you at the edge of the wood."

"Ah, that bit was tough. It was about as much as I could manage to put an image of me into your mind. It was becoming blocked by the fear, and I was in danger of losing touch with you. The blue mist wasn't easy, either."

Brendan pondered the prospect of losing touch with Annie. How on earth would he get home was the first question that presented itself. It didn't bear thinking about, and so he changed tack.

"I saw one of those demons before, in the wood when I was a kid."

"I know. They're rather sad creatures, really. They're very limited in what they can do without being commanded by a strong mind. You were something of a curio to them. Made their day I suppose, poor things."

Brendan felt mildly amused at the thought of those hideous creatures being the objects of anybody's pity, but he let the thought pass and looked about him.

They were sitting on the shores of yet another body of water, not so different from the one in Ireland. It was another sunny day and the placid surface reflected the blue sky with a solid, azure tonality of its own. The land on the far side was almost flat, and coloured a mixture of greens, browns and greys. To his left there was no land, the distant water making its own faint horizon with the infinite sky. To his right, at the far end of the lake, he could see randomly placed shapes that looked like dwellings backed by rising hills. He turned around and saw those hills climb steeply into statuesque mountains. They looked harsh, impregnable and forbidding. The area close to the lake was calm and felt peaceful, but beyond it this landscape was grander than the Irish one. He was sure he recognised it.

"Are we in Scotland?"

"Yes, on the west coast. This is a sea loch."

"Is this in my world or yours?"

"Neither. We're in a parallel universe to the one you live in."

Brendan's mouth fell open.

"What, one of those things the quantum scientists talk about?"

"More or less. You'll find it very familiar here, though. The vibrations are the same as yours. You'll function the same as you do at home, apart from any odd little advantages I might be able to give you."

Brendan blew out a breath between his lips.

"You know, life used to be so simple. Just me and my physical body, living in a physical world that was nice and predictable. I knew what I could do and what I couldn't do. I didn't have to worry about whether anybody could see me or not. If I bumped into a tree, I knew it would hurt. Nice, easy stuff like that."

His tone was reflective rather than rueful, but there was still a hint of sympathy in Annie's question.

"Is it too much? Do you want to give up the journey? Do you want me to take you home?"

"No."

"Good. So stop complaining."

Brendan smiled.

"OK. So what are we doing here?"

"We've come to save somebody's life."

"Sounds impressive. Whose life?"

"A young woman who's a supporter of mine. She's one of a rare breed with the sight who can see me. Most people here can't, just as they can't in your world."

"Do you come here a lot, then?"

"Quite a lot. Most parallel universes have a version of me already in them, just as they have a version of you, but this one took a slightly different course so I like to come and have a change of scene sometimes."

"Is that allowed?"

"Allowed by whom?"

"I dunno, whoever says what you can and can't do, I suppose."

"There is nobody. I can do whatever I want as long as I don't try to break the laws of nature. They're universal, but there's nobody controlling them. They just are, and I'm a part of the natural process, so it wouldn't be in my interest to break them. I would suffer if I did."

"Suffer how?"

"By losing my power, of course, through natural process."

There was that question again: just who, or what, was Annie? He felt she'd given him several clues, but the knowledge to interpret them was inadequate. The clues weren't enough to give him a definite answer yet, but he was beginning to have his suspicions. He felt a barrier fall across his train of thought, and it shifted to something she'd said earlier.

"You said we'd gone through a time shift. Do you mean we've gone back in history?"

"Not exactly. We're in a parallel world to yours, but the parallels aren't always perfect. Time proceeds at a slightly different rate here, and it's the equivalent of nearly three hundred years earlier than where you're at. That's why the jump from one universe to the other required a time shift. If we hadn't done that, this place would be empty of all life. It's also why we can rescue the woman. Everything you're going to see happened in your world in the seventeenth century, and the woman died. Obviously, we couldn't go back and save that version of her, but we can save this one."

"Obviously? It isn't obvious to a mere mortal like me."

"It's simple enough. You can't change history. If you managed to go back and alter something, that would just create another parallel universe. The original one would carry on unchanged. But this isn't history, so we're not changing it."

Brendan decided not to ask any more questions. This was something else that would have to be given careful consideration in due course.

"So what do we do?"

"We have to go to the village over there, but we have to keep out of sight."

"Can they see us, then?"

"They can't see me or Rabbit, but they can see you."

"Can they?"

"Of course. The whole plan depends on it."

"You have a plan, then?"

"Up to a point, although I daresay we might have to improvise here and there."

Brendan began to have reservations.

"You say they can see me?"

"Yes. Their vibrations are the same as yours. This is a normal, physical world to you. Be careful you don't bump into any trees."

Brendan failed to appreciate the humour.

"So they could hurt me as well. They could even kill me."

"Yes, they could; but they won't. Just think of the advantages you have over them. You can survive under water for as long as you need to, you have me on your side capable of doing some spectacular things with water, and you can hear my instructions, which they can't. Just stay close to the water, follow my instructions and trust me. I won't let them hurt you. If things turn dangerous, just jump into the water and I'll have us back to a safe place before they can react.

"Now, if you're ready, let's be moving. I can feel the poor woman having the ropes tied around her neck already."

Annie stood up and Brendan followed. They walked around a wall of rock and crossed a stony track that he assumed led to the village. A tract of Caledonian Pine came close to the road on the far side, and continued for some way up the slope that formed the base of the nearest mountain. Annie made for the trees, with Rabbit keeping close to her heels and looking around alertly. Having walked far enough to be out of sight of the road, she turned and followed a parallel course.

"This will bring us to within yards of the mill pool," she said. "They grow cereal crops in the small glen over there, to supplement the fish catches. My presence actually helps their crops to grow, if only they knew it. The mill pool is where they carry out their hideous ritual. That's where we're headed."

"So, what's the story? Who is this woman, and what's going to happen to her?"

"As I said, she's a supporter of mine and they're going to kill her for it."

"Yes I know, but what's she done exactly. What's the charge?"

"Being a woman."

"Is that all?"

"Not quite: being a woman and knowing more about how things work than they do."

"You're being enigmatic."

"I know. I'm angry. OK, we've got a few minutes; let me give you the full story. A long time ago a man went about preaching a message of peace, love and reliance on the workings of the universe. He tried to teach them that the God they should be following wasn't a separate being living in some place called heaven, but was the essence of a single, supreme consciousness of which they were all indivisible parts. His message was radical, and was hopelessly misconstrued. All his teachings about karma and rebirth were conveniently blocked out, as was his acceptance of the equality of women. The male-dominated culture of the time relegated the women to minor, and often tainted, roles.

"The men protected their dominance fiercely, and turned an enlightened message into a religion filled with bigotry, hypocrisy, and the pursuit of worldly power. Freedom of spirit was replaced with harsh, arbitrary, and often irrational rules and dogma. Obedience was everything. Spirituality became a simple contest between a single God and his enemy, the Devil. Any transgression of the rules was defined as heresy, and punished accordingly – usually with the most hideous cruelty. Women were particularly at risk, since their natures tend to make them more receptive to the harmonies and laws of the natural world. They could be easily defined as evil, and that suited the men who were in charge of things."

Brendan had been watching Annie's face during her eloquent diatribe. He'd seen the set of her jaw become firm, and her hard Gaelic eyes grow even harder. Her body had taken on a rigid, determined countenance. She was certainly angry, that much was obvious; and seeing her like that was a new experience. She continued.

"And what really gets me about these stupid hypocrites is that they've convinced themselves of their moral superiority. Morals! Shall I tell you about morals, Brendan?"

Annie seemed intent on continuing unchecked, whether Brendan wanted to be told about morals or not, but a brief pause ensued when they heard an indistinct sound nearby. Annie held up a hand and they all stopped. She looked at Rabbit, who looked back seemingly unconcerned. Annie relaxed and they continued walking, but the respite gave Brendan the opportunity to have his own say for once.

"I'm not very keen on morality, myself," he said. "I think morals are a measure of human weakness."

"Really?" said Annie. "Go on."

"Well, the way I see it is this. Morals are a set of loose diktats constructed according to an arbitrary perception of right and wrong in any given culture, and are usually determined by an equally arbitrary interpretation of a particular religion. They vary from culture to culture, religion to religion, and time to time. They're essentially man made, and are there to help preserve order among a population too easily swayed from the true guide to behaviour, which should be ethics. Ethics are universal. If the human being has the strength to be true to his inherent ethical sense, he wouldn't need morals. What's more, he would have the good sense and strength to resist those who seek to abuse and control through the imposition of so-called 'moral values.' It's quite ridiculous that a prostitute should be ostracised and called 'immoral,' whilst a man who makes weapons to kill people with – and gets rich on the profits – should be regarded as a good, upstanding citizen."

Brendan felt the bit between his teeth, and was glad of the free rein to gallop along the path of a favourite hobby horse. Annie merely said

"Brendan, I do believe you've got it. I think you might enjoy this little job."

Annie's reference to the "little job" brought Brendan back to the matter in hand, and he felt a thrill of apprehension.

"Hang on a bit," he said. "Don't you think I ought to know more about this woman? What's she done, what's going to happen, and how are you planning to deal with it?"

"She's a victim of their warped perceptions and their even more ridiculous logic. She knows me, and she knows that my presence is beneficial to the harvest. She also knows that I dwell in water, so she began the habit of throwing offerings into the river where it empties into the loch. A handful of corn, a few flowers, that sort of thing. She always did so in secret after dark, but a fishing boat was coming home late one night. The clouds cleared the full moon and they saw her. Needless to say, she was hauled off and accused of consorting with demons. They knew who she was making the offering to, because they still know something of the old ways. That was condemnation enough, since they regard me as a demon.

"They're such hypocrites, you know. Some of the men had been willing enough to accept my favours, but convinced themselves they'd been the unwilling victims of bewitchment. So, when some bits of brutal and perverted treatment – which they enjoyed, of course – didn't produce the required confession, she was condemned to a trial by water. You know the technique. They'll tie a rope around her and throw her into the mill pond. If she floats, she's guilty; if she sinks and drowns, she's innocent. If she doesn't drown, she'll be burned to death. Either way it's an execution."

Brendan had heard of the infamous trial by water, but it had always been a matter of faraway history to him. Being in a place where it was currently practised made him nervous.

"So what are we going to do?"

"We're going to have some *fun!*"

Annie emphasised the word with gleefully, and then glided and pirouetted for a few seconds, apparently revelling in anticipation of sublime revenge.

"We're going to teach them a lesson, Brendan."

"Are we, now? The 'we' bit is worrying me. What do I have to do?"

"Rescue her."

"Oh, right. That sounds easy enough!"

"Brendan, you're giving me a look I don't much care for. Don't you have faith in my abilities?"

"Certainly I do; It's mine I'm not so sure of."

Annie shook her head and tutted.

"You'll be fine. Just do everything I say and we'll give them the shock of their lives."

"Tell me, is this about saving the woman or beating up the men?"

"Both; why not?"

They were approaching the end of the wood, and could see the mill pool a short way across a patch of open ground. They could hear voices, too, little more than a low hum coming from a bend in the road where it curved around a rocky outcrop. And then the voices became louder as they watched a procession wind its way around it, heading for the pool. Brendan counted six men dressed in what he recognised as the black attire of seventeenth century Puritans. The man at the head was carrying a pole, on which was mounted a plain cross. A woman dressed in a simple calico dress was shuffling along in the middle of the group. She had two ropes tied around her neck, one being held tight by the man in front of her, the other by the man behind. The two of them pulled their ropes in unison at one point, clearly causing the woman some pain, for she lifted her head sharply and gasped a shrivelled cry. Annie gasped with her. The two men evidently found it amusing.

"Time to go into action," said Annie. "Keep low; they mustn't see you."

She walked quickly across the open ground. Brendan followed, stooping low so as to be out of sight of the procession. Annie knelt by the edge of the water and pulled Brendan close.

"Open," she instructed. Brendan dutifully took his lungful of elixir. "Right, we're going in. They'll take the neck halters off and tie another rope around her waist, then they'll throw her in. The first thing you have to do when she sinks down to us is untie the rope. Got that? Then we wait until they get to the bit in the prayer where they ask God to give them the sign. Then the pyrotechnics begin."

"Pyrotechnics? Fire isn't your element; water is."

"Don't be pedantic," she snapped. "I mean that's when the show begins. As soon as you've untied the rope, hold the woman in your arms, ready to carry her out. Make sure she doesn't float to the surface."

"But all that could take ages. Won't she drown?"

"Of course not. Do you think I'd let her drown? Start thinking straight, Brendan. We have a job to do."

Annie's voice was harsher than he'd ever heard it, and he had to make a conscious effort not to react to her sharp manner. She continued.

"While you're holding her, get ready for the water to part. Then I'll tell you what to do."

"Part? You mean, as in the Red Sea?!"

"Exactly."

"You're kidding!"

"I don't kid in this situation, Brendan. I've only ever done that trick once before, but there's no limit to what I can do with water when I'm angry. Come on."

They slipped into the pool and made their way to a point beneath the walkway that ran over the sluice gate. As they waited, Brendan mused on the different Annie he was now witnessing. All traces of softness had gone; she was no longer playing the role of a little girl. The physical appearance was still there, but she had the air of an authority figure; a mature woman who demanded immediate and absolute obedience. She looked at him coldly for a moment, and then looked up again.

Soon the sound of voices penetrated the water, and shapes appeared through the murk of the deep mill pond. The words were unintelligible to Brendan, whether because they were being filtered by the water, or because they came from a foreign language, he couldn't tell. He heard Annie's voice clearly, though.

"The language they're speaking is similar to Gaelic. When you get close to them, don't say anything. They'll take your garbling as indicating demonic origins. Understand?"

Brendan's spirits weakened. Annie was treating him like a lackey, and the thought of getting close to the men on the bridge was daunting, but he nodded his assent.

"Get ready," continued Annie. "Here she comes."

A dark shape appeared suddenly above them, and then the view was shattered as the surface was broken by the woman's plunging body. She sank to their level in a second, and Annie moved towards her. Brendan looked into her eyes. They were staring at Annie, full of shock, fear and disbelief. She let out a burst of life giving air from her lungs, and a mass of bubbles rose to the surface.

"Undo the rope – quickly."

Brendan did so. The knot was a simple one and easily untied. He looked back to see Annie cradling her mouth to the victim's. She released it and smiled at the woman. The fear had left her eyes. She evidently felt the change taking place within her, and a half smile of amazement and acceptance lit up her pale face.

"Now take hold of her," commanded Annie. "You'd better be up to carrying her when the water parts."

Brendan placed his right arm under the woman's knees, and his left under her back. It seemed she understood, for she wrapped her own arms about his neck and looked into his eyes, her own still full of wonder. They waited for several minutes, and Annie used the time to give him the next set of instructions.

"When the water parts, walk over to the far side of the pool. The water will come back together and you'll feel yourself lifted by it. That's because I'll be underneath holding you. You'll be able to step straight onto the bank, where you can put the woman down. That'll save you having to carry her too far. When you get onto the bank, walk with her to the men on the bridge and follow my next instruction. Whatever you do, don't show a hint of fear. Be in charge. They have to believe you're on God's side. Got that?"

"Yes."

Annie seemed to be listening to the words coming from above; Brendan felt a growing sense of apprehension. He was conscious of being about to face as stern a test as he'd ever encountered, and feared he might not be up to it.

"Yes you will. Believe in me."

He felt suddenly strengthened. With Annie he could do anything. He felt connected to her, bonded in a way he'd never known before. He was witnessing another side to her multi-faceted nature. He had experienced her cold, inscrutable side; he had seen her being gentle, compassionate, charming, friendly and humorous. Now she was showing him strength and determination. She stiffened and said

"This is it. Here we go."

Her body began to glow and ripple with the array of blues he'd come to associate with her. The little frock had gone and been replaced by an almost formless shimmer, dazzling in its intensity. He turned away, ready to begin his walk, and soon saw the sights of the open air. The water level was dropping rapidly around him and building up on either side. When it cleared his feet he began to walk slowly to the far side. There was no sound from the men on the bridge; he assumed they were struck dumb with wonder. He decided he should walk slowly and with authority, since he was now conscious of playing a role. He heard Annie's strained voice.

"Don't walk too slowly. I can only hold this for so long."

Fortunately, the young woman was small and undernourished. Her weight was easily carried and Brendan felt a thrill of achievement as he came close to the far bank. The men broke into an excited chattering, and he heard Annie's voice again.

"Good. They're debating who you are and how you're going to get out. Some think you're an angel, some a demon. The man with the cross is the one we have to work on. He's saying that the water parted when they asked God for a sign, so that means you must be one of the good guys. Spread your legs a little to help your balance."

The water began to rush back in and Brendan felt himself being lifted with the level. He could feel Annie's hands holding his feet. As soon as the surface was flat again, he stepped easily onto the bank and set the woman on the ground.

"Now for the difficult bit," he whispered under his breath.

He took the woman's hand and began the slow walk along the bank, returning the men's astonished gaze steadfastly and with pretended authority. The young man with the cross said something to the rest, who looked first at him and then at each other without reply. The walk was short, and Brendan was soon on the bridge and approaching the silent group of men. He began to worry. He was within a few yards of a group of men to whom killing was a religious duty. What should he do now? Annie's voice rang clear in his head, and right on cue.

"Concentrate on the man with the cross. Get up close to him, face him with authority, and smile - angelically!"

Brendan did so, fearing that his nervousness might make the angelic smile less than convincing.

"Now take hold of the cross and kiss it."

Brendan did that too, and the bearer fell to his knees, his face creased with a curious mixture of fear and rapture.

"Good. He's convinced. Now get ready for some more action. Whatever you do, don't look surprised."

His peripheral vision registered a strange sight. Several plumes of water rose from the mill race above the sluice, and remained stationary like so many glass columns. He consciously avoided looking at them, but continued to smile benignly at the kneeling figure. After a few seconds, pregnant with the silent wonderment of the men on the bridge, the plumes turned at right angles, becoming jets of immense power that swept the remaining five men into the mill pool. He heard a girlish giggle in his head, before the instructions continued.

"Two of the men can't swim, but the others will get them out all right. Now, point to the woman and then point at that kneeling idiot. Then put your hands together, as if in supplication. OK, good. Now gesture to him to help his comrades out of the water."

Brendan was enjoying his role, and made the most of Annie's instructions. Things were going well and his fear had vanished. It was beginning to feel like fun. The man nodded vigorously, and then hurried unsteadily off the bridge to help his spluttering and bemused companions. As soon as the attention of all six men was diverted, Annie spoke again.

"Jump into the mill pool."

Brendan couldn't resist giving way to a sudden urge first. He kissed the young woman on the forehead, and patted her cheek gently. He was almost beside himself with euphoria. She looked back at him with the same gaze of disbelief, but this time it was suffused with gratitude.

"Good luck," he said, feeling sure she would understand the sentiment if not the words. And then he jumped.

He was surprised to see the water part again just before he made contact, and then it closed over his head silently.

"They won't know how you disappeared if they didn't hear a splash," said Annie. "I like a neat finish."

"Do you think she'll be OK?" asked Brendan as they waited for the men to be clear of the water and make their way back to the village.

"No doubt of it. They were well convinced of divine intervention, and they'll leave her alone now. They fear the wrath of God will come upon them if they harm her again. They even feel they've learned a lesson, but whether that will stand the test of time, I don't know. I doubt it, somehow; old habits die hard. Still, they got a good shock and a good ducking, and the woman was saved. Well done, Brendan, very well done."

Brendan felt mightily pleased with himself, and he felt safe now. A thought suddenly intruded on his self-congratulation.

"Where's Rabbit?" he asked.

"In the wood. She keeps her distance when I'm in that kind of mood. She doesn't like it. I'm going to check if the coast is clear. Stay put."

Annie rose out of the water and left Brendan awaiting her instruction.

"They've gone. You can come out now."

Brendan lifted himself clear of the pond and stood up.

"Come on, better get back to the wood," said Annie.

They hurried across the open ground and entered the trees. It wasn't until they were safely out of sight that Brendan stopped looking around anxiously to be sure he hadn't been seen. He was encouraged by the sight of Rabbit hopping unconcernedly ahead of them. A warm sense of relief swept over him, and a welcome note of relaxation came with it. He looked at Annie, the little girl who had just commanded him sternly through a potentially dangerous adventure. He was hoping to see a return to the calm and friendly child he had grown used to. What he actually saw astonished him.

The top of Annie's head was now on a level with his shoulder. Her hair was still black and hanging long and loose, but it had a lustre about it that he hadn't seen before. The short, sleeveless frock had been replaced by a pristine white robe. It rippled as she walked, more elegantly than before, he thought. She looked back at him and he saw the biggest difference of all. Her eyes had lost some of their hardness. They had taken on a maturity that spoke of more advanced years, and yet they looked even stronger. There was a radiant, youthful beauty about her face. He stopped, and Annie turned to face him.

"You've grown," he said blankly.

"No, I haven't." Her tone was firm, but pleasant. "I'm just letting you see me a little more closely, that's all. I'm pleased with the way you conducted yourself today. I felt you'd earned a promotion. I was a bit sharp with you, wasn't I? Don't take it personally. There was a job to be done and I was angry.

Let's go and sit by the loch for a while. There'll be nobody about at this time of the day."

Brendan remained silent on the walk back. Annie said nothing either. Rabbit looked back and forth between them a couple of times, but seemed unconcerned. When they reached the water's edge, Annie reclined gracefully on a rock and stared at the horizon. Brendan was still intrigued by the change in her.

"Dare I make a comment?" he asked.

Annie looked at him without replying. Despite her still youthful appearance, her pointed gaze was both beguiling and uncompromising. There was an undoubted firmness about it; she was in control, but she was allowing him his comment.

"You have the appearance of somebody about to blossom into beautiful womanhood."

Annie lifted one eyebrow, and remained silent.

"Is this how you appear to other people?"

"Let that remain a mystery, Brendan. Can't have you learning everything at once, can we? How would you like a rest after your exertions? I think you've earned that, too. Let's go to a quiet place where there are no threats, eh? You can sleep again on the way, but don't worry; there won't be any time shifts on this trip. You won't slip away from me."

The prospect sounded good, and he nodded.

"Let's give you a lungful, and then we'll be off."

Brendan felt a fleeting sense of unease as Annie's mouth closed on his. He pushed the unwelcome sensation away immediately and focused on the practical purpose. Rabbit was the first to leap in as usual, and then the two of them walked into the gently lapping water. It closed over their heads and Brendan's world went dark.

Eden

Soon after losing consciousness, Brendan had a brief but very powerful dream. He saw Annie floating in front of him, her white robe rippling gently in a soft breeze that he felt was blowing from the beginning of time. The shifting white tones sometimes grew to such dazzling intensity that he had to shield his eyes from them, especially when she came up close and placed her hands either side of his temples. He felt his head begin to shake, as though it were being invaded by some strong but benevolent charge of electricity. Nausea and dizziness followed. The feeling gathered strength until it seemed that his body was about to be turned inside out. Pressure grew in every fibre of his physical and mental being, threatening to overwhelm him. And then it stopped abruptly.

He was left feeling so weak that a butterfly could have pushed him to the ground as surely as a bull elephant. He hung in the air helplessly, awaiting whatever fate might befall him. It surprised him that no fear sat alongside it. There was only the certain trust of a new born infant being held aloft by the strong arms of its mother. He was laid gently onto something soft, and then slipped contentedly back into an undisturbed sleep.

He awoke to the sight of a lilac sky and a pale yellow orb that could only be the sun. He heard noises to his left, and raised himself a little on one elbow. He turned to see Annie and Rabbit playing a game. They were on a beach. Annie was trying to shower Rabbit with handfuls of sand, while Rabbit was running, twisting and turning, and occasionally kicking sand back with her powerful hind paws. Annie was laughing joyfully, although the sound was feeble and indistinct to his half slumbering senses. Rabbit pressed her ears hard against her back as she ran, and then flicked them vertically when she stopped to feint one way or another. Brendan watched them for several minutes until he felt his strength returning. He raised himself further and looked around.

The beach was smooth and unblemished, except for the small patch disturbed by his playing companions. The look and feel of the sand astonished him. It was a deep golden yellow, and had the texture of sifted flour. A gentle swell of purple-blue water idly lapped the shoreline, flowing and fading with the rhythm of a lullaby trying to coax him back to sleep. His eyes flickered briefly until a growing awareness reminded him that he was in another world somewhere. Excitement roused his dull mind, and he sat up.

He looked out to sea, and saw a flock of white birds apparently playing their own game with a creature that looked like a dolphin. It leapt out of the water at intervals and tried to nudge the feet of a bird that was hovering just a little out of reach. Occasionally the bird would misjudge its approach, and the dolphin would catch it and then release its grip before it re-entered the water. Brendan watched them with growing fascination for some time. He turned around and marvelled at the heavy, dark green foliage growing in profusion at the top of the beach. Trees having the appearance of small palms sprouted above it at regular intervals, their branches seemingly laden heavily with fruit. He assumed he was on a tropical island, and it seemed a perfect place to rest.

A sudden scampering sound intruded and he felt a weight land on his lap. Rabbit laid her front paws on his chest.

"How are you feeling, Bren?"

"Great. Never better. This is a fabulous place. Where are we?"

Rabbit looked to one side, and then turned back.

"Better let the boss do the talking."

Annie walked over and knelt beside him. She folded her hands in her lap.

"Do you feel all right, Brendan? Did you have any dreams?"

"Ah, I thought it was probably more than just a dream. What was going on?"

"I had to change your vibrations. I know it wasn't pleasant having every cell in your body realigned. It's almost like being conceived and born all over again, but it was necessary. This place is so far away from your world that you wouldn't have been able to experience it otherwise."

"Where are we?"

"Paradise. At least, that's about the best word to sum it up. It was a glimpse of this place that led the early Bible writers to their description of the Garden of Eden. Only there's one big difference; there's no Adam and Eve here. There are no people at all. This is a seminal world, out of which others developed."

"It feels peaceful."

"So it should. That's why I brought you here for a rest. This place defines peace. Peace is all there is. There are animals, birds, fish, insects, trees, and flowers here. And there's food in abundance. No living creature eats any other living creature. They don't need to; they wouldn't know how to. They eat the food provided by the plants; they breed, and they play. It's a beautiful, innocent world."

"Why are there no humans?"

"Humans were added later. It was when people were introduced to other versions of this place that things changed. They were the most advanced species; they were given the knowledge that growth could be accomplished but, as I told you before, they misinterpreted that knowledge. They ignored the greater sense of spirit, and trapped themselves in material perception. They became dissatisfied; they wanted more. And so they became acquisitive. They began to hunt and kill the animals to have something different to eat. They began to fight and kill each other in pursuit of territory and status. They developed the need to be superior. And they changed the whole vibrational matrix so that everything else was affected too. And paradise was lost."

"Forever?"

"Effectively, yes. Like every other aspect of material existence, this place is just an illusion. This was the first illusion. There would be no point in going back to it. The only way is up, and the only true 'up' is out of the illusion."

"To seek oblivion and rejoin the Universal Consciousness?"

"That's it."

"It's a big ask."

"I know. A few people have done it."

"So are you saying there's no God, no heaven?"

"Of course there's a God; it's the definition that people get wrong. God can't be adequately understood or described in human terms. I would say that the very greatest of all human failings is to see God as a separate, supreme being sitting in heaven; an imagined father figure who orders the universe, watches them, judges them, and smites their enemies. I know you've gone beyond that, but you're still human so I can't tell you exactly what God is. The closest I could get would be to say that God is the essence of everything; God is love; God is the Universal Consciousness - the Supreme Intelligence of which every individualised being's intelligence is a tiny part. We're all part of God. Somebody said that all material existence is God's dream. That isn't such a bad description. And a few more enlightened people don't use the term God at all; they call the phenomenon the Is. That's closer to the truth."

"And it avoids the use of gender."

"Of course. There is no gender at that level. The idea is absurd."

"And heaven?"

"Heaven is a state of mind, the state of unbridled joy when all illusions and notions of separateness are removed"

Brendan looked away for a moment, pondering the paradoxical thought that the beauty he saw around him was only a pale reflection of what he might experience in emptiness. That, he had already realised, was what the man had shown him in the wood all those years ago.

He looked back at Annie who was regarding him in a way he hadn't seen before. Her young eyes had a motherly tenderness about them, and her mouth carried a faint smile. He was momentarily washed by a sense of profound beauty that her presence instilled in him. It seemed he was gleaning the first glimmers of the infinite - an understanding of true beauty, one that was supremely innocent and untrammelled by appearances, conditions, evaluations, or comparisons.

"How do I get there?" he asked earnestly. "What about the question of religion?"

"All religions offer hints as to how to get there, and some are better than others. The problem is seeing through the dogma that keeps people trapped in the illusion. Religions are man-made, and man-made institutions have a habit of eventually descending into reliance on dogma. And the more people they draw into their web, the more powerful they become and the more that power comes to matter. Eventually they build about themselves a delusion even further removed from the true nature of reality than the illusion they should be exposing. Some of their adherents have realised this down the centuries, but most haven't. The majority have always prevailed and the delusion has grown stronger. You don't need religion, Brendan. All you need do is accept the illusion in full knowledge of what it is. Live it; take pleasure in the little things; relax and let the road come to you."

Brendan looked fondly at Rabbit, still stretched out on his chest. He stroked her ears.

"You're a little thing, aren't you? What more could I want?"

Rabbit sat up, looked long into Brendan's face, and then at Annie. She leapt off her resting place and raced up the beach, her white tail soon disappearing into the undergrowth.

"She wants you to see the island," said Annie. "Care for a bit of rather lovely illusion?"

They stood up and followed Rabbit's paw prints. Pushing through the waist-high foliage was easier than he'd expected. The leaves were soft, luxuriant and yielding. There were no tangles or hard, woody growths to get through, and the palm fronds whispered as they swung contentedly in the warm breeze.

The land climbed for maybe a mile, but Brendan felt no fatigue. It seemed the air here was so full of life-giving energy that he could have climbed for ever. Emerging on the other side, he looked out over the plain of a river valley. It was some way in the distance, and misty; but he could see the flickering light on the flowing water as it ran its certain course to the ocean. The mist was sunlit, infused with a gentle shade of light gold, and the silhouettes of countless trees stood out in yellow-grey half tones in the distance. Shrubs of many sizes and shapes punctuated the shallow slope ahead of him. They displayed an abundance of coloured flowers, or so it seemed.

"They're not flowers; they're fruit," said Annie. "There's no shortage of food in this place."

"Can we just sit and look at it for a while?"

"Of course, as long as you don't tell me it's beautiful."

Brendan smiled at the recollection, and saw Rabbit ambling up close. She stopped and began to nibble a few blades of grass. He watched her with a frown, and asked Annie a question.

"Why is Rabbit eating grass? I thought she didn't need to eat."

Rabbit stopped eating and stared at him. Annie said nothing. Brendan turned to her, and saw an amused, questioning look on her face. And then he felt a sharp pain in his right big toe.

"Ouch!"

He looked in astonishment at Rabbit.

"You bit me!"

"Yes, I did."

"Why?"

"Because if you want to know why I'm eating grass, why not ask *me* why I'm eating grass?"

Brendan's indignation was immediately tempered by a reluctant acknowledgement of guilt.

"Sorry! OK, why are you eating grass?"

"Because it tastes nice."

"Right, fair enough! But you didn't have to bite me!"

"Suppose not. It didn't hurt too much, did it?"

"Yes, it did. It's still throbbing."

He rubbed it pointedly to emphasise the fact. Rabbit rushed away and disappeared into the undergrowth. She re-emerged quickly, holding a large leaf in her mouth, which she placed into Annie's outstretched fingers.

"Take your shoe and sock off," Annie ordered.

Brendan did so, and Annie wrapped the leaf around his throbbing toe. The pain disappeared in seconds.

"This place provides all the animals need," she said. "Don't forget, they are physical like you. They can get injured, so nature provides a cure for everything. The leaves of that bush over there stop any bleeding; that one just below it knits broken bones; the stems of that big one over there cure any sort of bacterial infection, and so on. You just need to know which ones do what, as the animals all do."

"I've heard it said that the same is true of earth."

"Almost, but earth isn't quite as perfect as this place."

"So answer me the big question, then. Was this place created or did it evolve? Are we to believe Darwin or the Creationists?"

"Both. The illusion of material existence was engendered by the Universal Intelligence, and it contained the mechanism for development and adaptation. There is no conflict. That argument is typical of the foolishness that pervades human society. Blind religious bigots on one side, blind scientific bigots on the other; and all of them certain that they're right. Arguing seems to give them a sense of their own importance. They're all too silly to waste time thinking about. Fancy a walk?"

They stood up and began a leisurely stroll downhill towards the estuary. They walked between bushes and small trees, none of which were recognisable to Brendan's modest knowledge of botany, but all of which bore fruits, nuts or berries that were not so different to those he was used to.

"Try one," said Annie.

Brendan selected one that had caught his attention. It was the colour of a strawberry, the shape of a raspberry, and the size of a medium apple. He bit into its succulent flesh and let out a murmur of approval. It had the taste of a strawberry, but richer and sweeter.

"There's one over there you might find interesting," continued Annie.

They walked to the edge of a wood, in which nearly every tree had fruit hanging from its branches that looked like pale brown pears. Brendan picked one and took a bite. The flesh was firm and tasted like a combination of chicken and mushroom.

"That one is full of protein and carbohydrate," said Annie. "It's a particular favourite with the bigger animals. Talking of which, look."

Brendan froze. Standing only a stone's throw away, a magnificent big cat was watching him with apparent interest. It was pure white, and reminded him of a Siberian tiger he'd seen in a zoo once. His fear was compounded by astonishment as a small deer walked between the trees and stood next to the cat. They both looked at Brendan for a few seconds, and then walked in tandem towards him. Annie's voice was reassuring.

"Don't be frightened. They're just curious. They won't hurt you."

The two animals came close to continue their inspection. Brendan's eyes were fixed on the tiger's, which were on a level with his own. They were strong, unafraid, and yet not fierce. The animal was massive, and he had a sense of powerful muscles rippling beneath the dense coat of hair. Both animals sniffed him from top to toe.

"You can touch them. They won't mind."

Brendan reached out tentatively. He stroked the deer's head with his right hand, and brought his left up to the tiger's neck. They felt soft and warm, and both reciprocated with a gentle movement of their heads. And then they turned and walked placidly away again. Brendan was transfixed; he felt humbled, and quite unable to speak for a while. Emotion welled up in his throat. He felt Annie's arm wrap around his own.

"Did you enjoy that?"

He nodded, fighting to keep his emotion in check. His voice was broken as he uttered the words he remembered so well from his Sunday School classes. They had been important in shaping his attitude to animals.

"The wolf also shall dwell with the lamb, and the leopard shall lie down with the kid."

"And the lion shall eat straw like the ox," added Annie. "Isaiah's prophecy was actually a statement of historical record, just as the story of Atlantis was not a historical fable, but a prediction of the future."

"Was it?"

"More of that another time. Let's walk down to the river. There are some seals down there playing a game of tag with the fish."

Brendan looked into Annie's mischievous eyes.

"You're having me on, aren't you?"

"Yes. Actually they're trying to persuade the crabs to help them with a game of tennis. They want the crabs to be the balls. Come on."

They walked side by side down the remainder of the slope that was now becoming rocky, and then sat in silence to enjoy the sunshine. The liquid babble of the running water was punctuated by a splash every so often as something silver leapt out of it briefly, and then disappeared again. A pack of animals resembling wolves walked sedately across the hill on the far side, accompanied by scampering young ones that seemed to have no other purpose in life than to play. A couple of the adults turned to look at Brendan at one point, but walked on unconcerned.

"This place really is paradise," he said. "How on earth did we ever manage to lose it? I think I'd be quite content to stay here for ever."

Annie's reply shocked him out of his reverie.

"If this is something like heaven, you're going to have to see hell too, I'm sorry to say. Got to have balance, so that's where we're going next. Well, not hell exactly, more purgatory."

Brendan's spirits sank.

"Do we have to?"

"It's part of the journey. You have to see all sides."

"Do we have to go so soon?"

"Not just yet; when the sun sinks. You're still weak from your recent experience, so have a sleep now. I'll wake you when it's time to leave."

Brendan was reluctant to sleep; it seemed such a waste when there was so much peace and beauty to experience. But he saw himself again as an infant, this time being gently laid into a cot and persuaded to take an afternoon nap. He was content to give himself to the role; it was, in a manner of speaking, largely what he amounted to in this situation. He felt amused by the thought that Annie should be singing a lullaby to him, and turned to smile at her. She lifted her eyebrows in response, and Brendan had no doubt that she knew exactly what he was thinking. He lay down and Rabbit nestled herself in the crook of his arm.

"No bad dreams this time, Bren," she said. "No need. Have a good sleep."

Hungry Ghosts

A gentle shake of the arm woke Brendan up. The sun had taken its leave for another day, and twilight had descended on Eden. The sky overhead had faded to a deep purple, but eased into vivid pink as it sank ahead of him onto the low hill beyond the river which now ran scarlet.

"How long have I been asleep?"

"Long enough," said Annie, whose robe appeared a soft shade of cerise in the evening light. "The sun has set. Are you ready to move on?"

Brendan sat up to see Rabbit silhouetted against the water. She seemed to have her back to him, and looked alert. He didn't feel ready to move on yet. The relentless diurnal imperative was, on this occasion, an irritation. He wanted to sit there and pass the warm, crimson twilight in contemplation and small talk.

"What did you do while I was asleep?"

"I watched you, and I learned about you. The energies of sleep can be most instructive. Then I talked to a bear who came to investigate the stranger in her land. Rabbit played a game with a snake. She likes it here."

"Who wouldn't? It's the sort of place you'd never want to leave; but I suppose we have to dive into some deep, dark place now, do we?"

"Yes."

"I don't suppose I'll ever see this place again, will I?"

"Yes, if you want to, but not with me."

"How can I come here without you?"

"When you die. You can create your own reality then, at least up to a point and for a certain time. If this is where you want to be, this is where you can be. Just keep the memory locked safely in your heart. You'll find it again when the time comes, if you still want to."

Brendan felt a sinking feeling again. Death seemed a long way off, and he didn't want to wait that long. He was consumed with a desire for peace, but all he saw was a succession of journeys stretching endlessly into an unknown future. Some might be of import, but most would be nothing more than a stolid trudge. He was conscious of looking too far ahead, and brought his mind back to the matter in hand. Journeys are about moving on, even if it means falling from paradise into a pit of unknown depth.

"If you say it's time to go, then so be it. Lay on Macduff."

"And damned be him who first cries 'Hold, enough.'"

"You know Shakespeare?"

"Of course. He knew me, too."

There was a mischievous look in her eyes. The old question leapt into his mind again, begging to be asked. He shook his head ruefully as she grasped his hand and lifted him to a standing position. All would be revealed, no doubt - eventually.

They walked to the water's edge and he took one final look at this Eden that was the first illusion. The dusk was falling rapidly, but he could still make out the detail of a perfect, primeval garden where peace and plenty ruled supreme. No sign of man's encroachment polluted so much as an inch of ground here, and the star-spattered sky above his head showed the way to countless other worlds. He was sure that the one they were heading for was much closer, and yet so very much further away. The paradox was beyond his mortal mind for the time being. He walked with Annie into the water, and soon they were diving deep into a dark ocean devoid of life.

Annie was holding his hand as they travelled downwards, ever downwards. Her form was only just visible in the murk, but he felt her hand grip his more tightly as she pointed ahead. A large piece of rock having the appearance of a miniature mountain stood on the sea bed, and a black circle was vaguely etched on the side they were approaching. He heard her voice.

"We're about to go in. A word of warning: this place isn't pleasant. Whatever you see in there, remember that nothing can touch you. And whatever you feel, don't give up hope. Trust me implicitly; you will come out unharmed. Ready?"

They rushed through at lightning speed, and soon emerged above the water. Brendan felt his feet rest on something hard. Rock, he assumed; and it was uneven, with jagged points and treacherous gullies. He stumbled several times as they walked up onto a foreshore shrouded in a damp, grey mist. Rabbit was waiting for them, but she wasn't scampering this time. She was sitting stock still and looking fretful; she even seemed to be shivering slightly.

"Are you OK?" he asked.

There was no reply.

"She's sensitive, said Annie. She knows there's nothing here that can hurt her, but this place drains sensitive minds. That's why you must focus on my strength and the trust you need to have in me."

Brendan was beginning to understand what she meant. He felt cold, even though he knew the sensation wasn't physical. The chill was deep inside him, trying to induce a shiver that he knew would be relentless if he gave in to its incessant tugging. Anxiety came with it, a sense of dread that was also inexplicable, since his rational mind was still content with Annie's assurances.

They walked a few yards into the empty mist until he saw another rock face and the entrance to a cave. The blackness within was impenetrable. There was no sound of any sort, not even the drip of water in what was, to Brendan, the dampest and dreariest place he had ever encountered.

"This feels even worse than the place where the demons were," he muttered, his words jerking and starting as he struggled to control the coldness in his chest.

"This is the worst place you'll ever see," replied Annie.

The sense of gloom and despondency was almost palpable. His mind sought a familiar reference, and he recalled an incident several years earlier, when he had disembarked at a closed railway station shortly after midnight on a freezing December night. The train had been delayed for several hours, and arrived at its destination long after the locking of the gates. He remembered the unearthly chill on the dimly lit, vaulted platform, and the patches of ice he could see out in the open air beyond it. He remembered the lone station attendant who had been forced to wait for the uncommon event of a train stopping there at that time of the night, and his surly countenance as he released the benighted passengers out into the empty street. That was what this place felt like: a cold, closed edifice where nobody had any right to be. A sense of intense loneliness engulfed him.

And then he heard a noise, a faint but regular splashing that grew in volume until it sounded close by. He looked around, seeking the source, and saw a dark shape drift across the line of his sight until it stopped at what appeared to be a kind of promontory. He strained his eyes until he made out the shape of a boat. A shadowy, indeterminate mass occupied the mid section, and two oars were shipped vertically. There was silence again, and Brendan turned to Annie with a whispered question.

"What's that?"

"In most cultures he's simply called The Ferryman."

"Who's he ferrying?"

"You'll see."

Brendan turned back to see a second shape apparently climbing out of the boat. The one sitting amidships held out an arm and pointed in their direction, and then began rowing backwards until the vessel's shady form was consumed by the mist. A sense of hopelessness and pernicious decay grew in Brendan as the figure walked slowly towards them. Fear sought to take hold, too, as it loomed larger and began to take shape. Soon it stood before him, staring blankly into the void. Brendan felt a thrill of horror and disgust attach itself to his despondency.

The figure had the overall appearance of a human, and yet there was something tragically inhuman about it. A thin, horribly emaciated torso with spindly arms sat on top of legs that were little short of skeletal. It had no clothes and no evidence of gender. It was a scrawny, humanoid lump, seemingly made of sweaty, black plasticine. Its skull reminded him of the heads of mummies he'd seen in museums – dry-boned and desiccated, from which all semblance of life has been removed. The notion that this creature might possess a degree of sentience disgusted him further; the possibility that it might come within touching distance was too awful to contemplate.

And then it turned its eyes directly at his. He was shocked to see that they shone bright green; but that shock was only a mild precursor of the horror to come. The creature opened its cadaverous mouth and emitted a wretched, desperate howl that sank into the surrounding air, becoming almost instantly muffled by the clammy mist. Brendan felt shaken rigid, as though the hideous sound had dealt him a paralysing blow. Annie's voice brought him back to a proper sense of his own life and identity.

"Move aside Brendan. Let it pass."

He looked round at her. He felt dazed and depressed, but she appeared quite unmoved by the sight of the creature.

"Move aside," she repeated.

He did so, and the source of his horror lurched unsteadily forward with its head bowed. It entered the cave and was soon swallowed by the darkness. He looked at Annie again. She was walking over to Rabbit, now leaning sadly against the rock face at the entrance to the cave. Her own head was bowed, and she reminded Brendan of the baby rabbit he had watched behind the croft in Ireland. Annie picked her up and cradled her fondly in her arms. He thought he heard a quiet sob, but whether from Annie or Rabbit he couldn't tell.

"I don't think we should stay here too long," said Annie. "Let's get this part of the trip over with."

Brendan had little will to speak. The darkness here was unremitting and there was no evidence of meaningful life. What could he possibly learn in such a place as this, and would there be any escape? A piece of his mind held firm, however, and he quietly asked the obvious questions.

"What was that creature, and what is this place?"

He hardly recognised his own voice; it sounded cracked, feeble and uncertain. Annie's reply had a hint of urgency about it.

"A place where we shouldn't waste time sitting around. I'll explain as we're walking."

"Walking where?"

"Through there," she said, pointing into the cave.

"I don't think I can," he replied. "Suppose we encounter that *thing* again. And there might be more of them."

"There are plenty more of them, but we have to go that way; it's the way out."

He looked into Annie's face. It was strong, determined and, best of all, in control. His spirits eased a little way out of the pit into which they had sunk.

"OK."

"Good. Hold onto my arm, and remember the two things I told you: nothing here has any power over you, and you mustn't give in to hopelessness. Let's go."

Brendan took hold of Annie's arm and looked at Rabbit. Her eyes were closed.

"I sent her to sleep. She's too innocent for this place."

They walked into the cave and were engulfed by the darkness. They were treading on hard but even ground, and Brendan heard Annie's voice.

"The answers to your questions now. This place is what the Catholics in your world call purgatory. Other cultures have different names for it; I favour the Tibetan one – the Hungry Ghost Realm, because that's what the creatures here are. They're spirits who are constantly hungry. They're hungry for food, but there is none. They're permanently cold, but they have no means of warming themselves. They want to see the light, but there is only darkness. They want to commune with their own kind, but they have no language. They even retain sexual desire, but they have no gender. They are all desperate to die, but they know they're already dead. It's about as wretched an existence as it's possible to imagine."

"They used to be human?"

"Oh yes, all of them."

"So what did they do that was bad enough to be sent here?"

"They weren't sent. Who would send them? They consigned themselves to this place by allowing their energies to fall so low, life after life, that they dropped out of the usual cycle of life, death and rebirth, and sank to a deeper level. There is nowhere else to go then but here. They're not people who simply had one bad lifetime as murderers or tyrants or habitual abusers, like the Mr Cooper you saw hanging in the wood. You know a bit about karma; you know that before you're born into each life you have some choice over how that life will proceed: what options you might be presented with, and how some of the consequences will balance out. Power in one life can be balanced by oppression in another. A prince is reborn a pauper. The celebrity becomes insignificant. That's normal progression. But those who blindly choose the ephemeral paraphernalia of self interest like wealth, power and fame time after time – and then pursue their obsessions with no regard for the interests of others - build up such a burden of negative karma that the balance comes all at once in one radical and profound consequence. They slip to the lowest level of the wheel and end up here."

"And do what?"

"Suffer, what else?"

"For ever?"

"No. Eventually the debt is paid off and they start all over again."

"How long does it take?"

"Time has no meaning in this situation. To them, it feels like an eternity."

"So why do I feel so wretched here?"

"Because you're surrounded by the energy of desperation and despair."

Brendan remembered the time he had gone for a job interview at a high security prison. He had felt something similar then. Even before reaching the appointed place for the interview, he'd decided not to accept the job. There was no way he could work surrounded by such an atmosphere of hopelessness and suffocating restraint. This was a million times worse.

He continued to hold Annie's arm tightly as he walked blindly beside her through the black tunnel. But then a small patch of dark grey became visible some way ahead. It grew bigger until they emerged onto a ledge. Beyond them lay an unremitting prospect of more darkness. There was no ground to walk on here, though. There was only empty space.

"Step off the ledge with me, but keep your arm locked in mine until you gain confidence. We can't fall; there is no gravity beyond the ledge. And we move by the power of will."

Brendan felt weak. Annie was his only hope, and he doubted he would ever release his grip on her arm again. He was totally at the mercy of her bidding, and stepped off the ledge as she did. They drifted forward into the darkness. At first they were alone, but then he saw a figure like the one he'd seen enter the cave. As far as he could tell in this hell without horizons, the creature was drifting forward too. He asked Annie whether it had a purpose, or whether it was moving aimlessly.

"It has a purpose," she said. "We're going to follow it."

The creature drifted on, it's arms and legs hanging loosely in the air and it's head bowed. Annie and Brendan kept station close behind. He saw another one a little way to the right, and then a third rising up from below. Soon a fourth appeared. It seemed they had a joined a growing convoy.

"They're new arrivals," said Annie. "This batch comes from your home town. That's why I chose this route. They can sense something – something they need. They don't know what it is yet, but they know it lies in that direction."

More floating figures appeared from every quarter, all heading for the same invisible destination. And then it took form in the distance. A speck of lighter grey appeared and grew rapidly until Brendan gasped. He recognised the town he had grown up in. House, shops, schools, factories – they were all there. But everything was grey and semi transparent. There was none of the colour or solidity that would make it truly alive. They were the ghosts of houses; this was a ghostly image of his town. As they moved closer he could see familiar life going about its business. Spectral people walked in the streets; spectral children played in the park; spectral vehicles drove up and down, as though playing their part in some devilish tableau. The creatures were heading into the midst of it.

"Is this place real, or some sort of projection?" asked Brendan.

"It isn't a projection. This is your world, your town; and it shows just how close other dimensions are to it."

They continued to follow the figure they had picked up initially. It headed for the first house at the end of a terraced street, and stopped when it reached the wall. It hung there for a second, and then appeared to press itself into the fabric of the brickwork. Brendan and Annie moved to the side of it, and also pressed themselves against the wall. The scene before them was brightly lit. A family of two adults and two children were sitting at a table eating a meal. A low, helpless moan came from the figure standing next to them.

"This is what they do," said Annie. "Some will watch people eating; some will try to get warmth and comfort from a fire; some will try to talk to the people. All in vain, of course. They soon learn that it's hopeless and become even more despondent.

"Only a small number of people have any sense at all of their presence. Those who do, the ones you might call psychic, find the experience frightening. Most of them just get a cold chill and a sense that there's something supernatural around. A few might see what looks like an inexplicable shadow on the wall, or a movement out of the corner of their eye. People used to be more attuned to this sort of thing; it's where a lot of ghost stories come from. But not these days. The creatures eventually accept the pointlessness of the exercise and retire to live out their time in the darkness."

They slid back from the wall, and the grey facsimile of a townscape stretched before them again. Brendan was fading. He felt sick, weak and hopelessly deflated. His sense of worth was gone; he was defeated. He was becoming one of the creatures and knew there was no hope left. His arm began to slip out of Annie's, until he heard her voice commanding him.

"Don't let go Brendan. You're not one of them. It's only the weight of their despondency that's making you feel like this. Hold on. Be strong. We'll soon be out of here."

Brendan's mind was torn. An overwhelming desire to give in was consuming every fibre of him, but he couldn't ignore Annie. She was strong, and not to be refused. And yet her power seemed to be growing distant. He had a mental image of her floating into the darkness and leaving him behind, even though the sensation in his arm was warm and real. It was still locked firmly around hers.

Some part of his mind snapped. Annie was a demon; she had lured him here in order to trap his soul in a dark prison without hope of release. She was the embodiment of evil. He railed at her, accusing her of the most terrible betrayal. He had been a fool ever to have trusted her. He knew now that the man in the wood had been the Devil all along. She was his consort, bent on doing his diabolical business. He burst into uncontrollable sobbing and screamed the most fearful, primal scream at her. He pushed at her, trying to remove her hideous presence from his sight.

She remained silent throughout his ranting. The expression on her face stayed calm as she looked back into his agonised eyes. She lifted her arm and pointed to Brendan's right shoulder. A fragment of his spirit re-ignited, and he followed her finger. A cadaverous creature was floating only inches away, its eyes searching every inch of his body. He felt too weak to recoil. Nausea rose from his stomach into his throat. The creature looked suddenly away from him and turned its attention to Annie. It shot forward with remarkable speed and stopped in front of her, repeating the inspection. Annie continued to look at Brendan. The creature lifted a bony hand and stretched a finger towards Rabbit. Her eyes opened as it was about to make contact. She screamed the same agonised scream he had heard from the baby rabbits, only much louder. She leapt from Annie's arm in panic, shooting into the darkness to Brendan's left.

Time shifted. Brendan's mind went into slow motion, and his thoughts became clear. Rabbit was leaping into the void where she would be at the mercy of countless prying eyes and prodding fingers. How long would it take to find and rescue her? Would they ever find her? The prospect was a terrible one, and he couldn't allow it. He reached out his arm and caught one of her hind legs, pulling her back to his chest and holding her firmly. Normal time reasserted itself, and with it came resolve and great anger. He moved to face the creature and felt his anger form into a wave of motive power capable of being directed. And directed it was. The creature tumbled away from him and disappeared into the darkness.

"That wasn't a very nice thing to do Brendan."

It was Annie's voice. She was smiling at him. He felt guilty for having committed an act of violence against something that was far below an animal. But then he remembered what he had said to her, and his guilt rose to fever pitch. He looked imploringly at her, searching for the words that would convey an adequate apology.

"No need," she said, smiling broadly. "It was just the proximity of the creature that was affecting you. I did warn you, didn't I?"

"You must hate me for my weakness – and those terrible insults."

"Not at all. For a human, you hung on pretty well. You're a lot stronger than you think, you know. I'd say it's time we left this place, wouldn't you?"

Rabbit leapt for a second time, out of Brendan's arms and upwards.

"You needn't have worried about her," said Annie. "She knows the way out of here. But she still loves you for rescuing her, even though I put her up to it in order to get your spirits back."

"You didn't!"

"I'm getting to know you, Brendan Bradshaw. I know what moves you. Take hold of my arm again."

He did so and felt giddy as they rose rapidly. He looked up to see a white patch high above. It turned pale blue as it expanded, gradually becoming richer as they drew nearer. They passed through it into clear blue water, and then emerged above the waves of a placid sea. A rocky shore stood a little distance away, and Rabbit was sitting on it. As soon as they left the water, she leapt into Brendan's welcoming arms.

"Thanks Bren. You did great down there. Horrible place, isn't it? You OK now?"

She looked into his eyes intensely, her cocked head indicating genuine concern. Brendan sank to his knees. He laughed uncontrollably and shed tears of relief, rocking gently with Rabbit held close to his heart.

Oracle

Rabbit hopped off to explore the rock pools while Brendan sat alone in silence, gathering his fractured spirits. He was looking out to sea, taking comfort in the regular movement of the waves and trying not to think of what he had just witnessed a little way beneath them. Annie sat apart, further up the rocky slope. He could feel her watching him, but he declined to turn round for several minutes. He could feel something else, too. Waves of warm energy flooded into his back and seemed to be massaging his heart, such was the tingling he felt in his chest. He knew where it was coming from, and he knew what its purpose was. Annie was healing him, and yet he felt unsure about his feelings for her. He wished she hadn't taken him to that terrible place. The memory of it still filled him with a horror that he knew he could never completely forget.

As his spirits recovered, however, a sensible clarity began to re-assert itself. It wasn't long before he trusted her completely again. He knew she hadn't taken him there gratuitously to cause distress, and he knew he had never been in physical danger. He still felt sorry for his pathetic outburst, and he was grateful that she had not held it against him. Most of all, the understanding grew in him that being with her was a privilege, and that the privilege would have to be matched by fortitude on his part. He realised that the purpose of a journey is not to be comfortable, but to accept and negotiate whatever it offers; and he realised that life itself is just one of many journeys. The memory of the bond he had felt with Annie came back, too. He was growing strong again, and turned to see her sitting only a few feet away. She looked pleased. She also looked different.

Her robe was now coloured a deep emerald green, with red borders on the hem and sleeves. Her hair was pulled back into a long pony tail, apparently held in place by a black velvet band from what little he could see of it. Something glinted at the base of her robe, and he saw a silver bracelet festooned with silver charms wrapped around her ankle and sitting demurely on her bare foot. Her face had matured further. He had been right in his earlier remark that she was about to blossom into a beautiful young woman. His prediction now sat before him, and her beauty was such as to seem almost unreal.

"You've grown again," he said.

She nodded and patted the rock next to her. He followed her bidding, despite feeling a sudden upsurge of inadequacy. He avoided looking into her face, but sat quietly for a few seconds gazing out over the sparkling sea. And then the question finally broke.

"You're a goddess, aren't you?" he said guardedly, keeping his eyes averted.

Annie laughed and pulled his face around so that their eyes met. What he saw there confused him. Her look was friendly, warm, maternal even; and yet there was still an undoubted distance about it - a space that he knew he was not allowed to cross. He wondered whether he would ever be afforded the honour.

"I dislike that term," she said. "Humans use it indiscriminately. Gods live in the god realm; they keep themselves apart. They're comfortable, superior, aloof. I'm not one of them, and I wouldn't know how to be. Don't expect to understand the whole of who or what I am yet; just treat me with respect. I trust you to define it in your own terms. You have wisdom as well as strength. I'm not a model of perfection, merely the spirit of a deeper level of reality. You'll find out more as we continue, which is what we should be doing, if you're ready."

Brendan continued to look into her deep blue eyes, now on a level with his own. He felt uncertain; he still felt inferior; and he understood that proper respect was a difficult quality to judge. The word "veneration" came into his mind. Was that respectful or sycophantic?

"Relax, Brendan," she said, earnestly leaning towards him. "If it helps, try to think of me as an esteemed older sister. That will do for now."

"That could be difficult. You look young enough to be my daughter."

"I'm showing you different aspects of who I am. You'll work it out eventually. Come on; Rabbit's getting impatient. Let's be showing you another world."

"Where are we?"

"Oh, this isn't the other world. Don't you recognise where we are?"

Brendan looked around. Blue sea, rocky foreshore, grassy slopes higher up with ragged bushes dotted about, a sun that was too bright to look at...

"Should I?"

"Yes. We're back in your world. This is a Greek island, and that's the Mediterranean Sea."

"Oh, right. So where's the other world?"

"The entrance to it is over that hill. Let's walk."

The slope was rocky at first, but easily manageable. Rabbit went on ahead, as was her way, and seemed to be playing hide and seek with them as they negotiated the shrubs higher up. They reached the top to see that the land fell away on the other side, running down to a plain with clumps of what appeared to be plantations dotted at regular intervals – olive groves, he assumed. A village sat in self-conscious isolation at the foot of the hill, but there was no sign of life.

"It's Sunday," said Annie, as though that explained everything. "It's the only village left here now. It used to be quite well populated at one time. There's a Roman amphitheatre a few miles away. People used to come here to visit the very place we're going to, but not any more."

"Why not?"

"They don't believe in that sort of thing these days."

"What sort of thing?"

"Questions, questions! Humans are so full of questions. Just wait and see. It's that way."

They walked along the ridge until it widened into a green plateau. Brendan could see that the land rose about a mile ahead, and was topped with a small range of low, rocky hills. They were heading in that direction, and soon reached the base where they had to start clambering over boulders and slippery scree. The going was more difficult here, but eventually they reached what appeared to be a deliberately constructed, earthen platform, now covered with well established, scrubby growth. What worried Brendan was the fact that it stood in front of a cave. Annie was turning to look at the land behind them as Brendan was about to express his misgivings.

"Just imagine it," she said. "Hundreds of people ranged all the way down the slope and beyond, while the chosen few were riddled with trepidation and standing right where we are."

That made Brendan feel worse. Was this a place of sacrifice, or something? Was he about to witness another vision of hell?

"Do we really have to go in there? Not another cave. I've developed a bit of an aversion to caves."

"But this cave is very different," she replied lightly. "Show him, Rabbit."

Rabbit ran enthusiastically into the aperture, disappeared for a few seconds, and then reappeared.

"Nothing bad in there, Bren. It's empty."

"So what is it?" he asked, turning suspiciously to Annie.

"It's a special place, a sort of holy place if you like. It's where the Oracle used to reside. It's empty now because the world has no place for Oracles any more."

"So what's the point of going in if it's empty?"

"I didn't say the Oracle no longer exists, did I? And it still provides a gateway to a world you'll be very privileged to see. Do you want to?"

"Of course."

They walked into what seemed a very ordinary cave. There was enough light to move about comfortably, and Rabbit was quite content to hop around examining every inch. The floor was bare earth, and the walls rose vertically from it until they curved to form a high ceiling. Only in one place was the smoothness of the wall interrupted. It lay in the darkest corner, and had been difficult to see until Brendan's eyes had accustomed themselves to the low light. The rock was worn away there, leaving a horizontal ledge about two feet across, and a recess big enough to accommodate a person. He assumed it was the repository of the Oracle. Annie nodded.

"Do you want to see her?"

Brendan's spirits had recovered sufficiently to allow a little of his accustomed levity.

"Does she bite?"

"Come here." Annie's voice was friendly, but firm.

Brendan walked to over to her. She was the same height as him now, and her face looked pale but radiant in the gloom.

"I have to change your vibrations again, but it won't be as bad as last time. Close your eyes; it will make the transition easier."

Brendan felt her fingers touch his temples again. There was only a hint of nausea this time, accompanied by a little dizziness and the brief sound of a rushing wind.

"You can open them again."

The cave looked ostensibly the same, although it seemed a little lighter and the ground felt slightly spongy. Annie took him by the hand and led him to within a few feet of the recess.

"Now we sit and wait."

They sat cross legged on the earth, with Rabbit between them. Annie placed the palms of her hands together in front of her chest and closed her eyes.

"Should I do that as well?" asked Brendan.

"Shh..."

There was nothing to see or hear for several minutes, and Brendan wondered how long his ageing knees would take the strain. They were fine so far. He wondered whether it was the change of vibrations that made him feel physically younger – more supple. That was interesting. He concentrated on the recess again, and heard the first stirrings of a sound that was difficult to identify. As it grew louder, he thought it sounded like the crackling of burning branches in a garden bonfire, but more regular. He mentally queried its source.

"Energy," said Annie. Brendan turned to see that her eyes were open. "Look."

Something was taking shape in the recess. It was grey, faint and swirling at first, but soon coalesced into a dark figure resembling a shrouded, seated person. He was shocked to hear a deep, female voice echo around the cave.

"You are welcome lady, but why have you brought me back here; and who is the human?"

"I asked you back for two reasons. Firstly, I ask you to grant access to the world apart. Secondly, the human is a traveller who has a question to ask."

"Ask."

"What?" said the confused Brendan. "Question? What question?"

"You wanted to know about Atlantis, remember? The Oracle can tell you."

"Oh, that. I just ask a simple question, do I?"

"Try."

Brendan cleared his throat.

"Did Atlantis exist once, or is it just a myth?"

The covered head turned in his direction. It appeared that the Oracle was looking at him, although no face could be seen, and a ripple of nervousness ran down his body. The answer was immediate.

"You are confused. You ask two questions. The answer to both is 'no.'"

Brendan was, indeed, confused. He looked at Annie and shrugged.

"The answer lies deeper," she said. "Try asking the first question again and she will explain."

"Did Atlantis exist?"

"Your question presumes the reality of time. There is no time. There is only being."

Brendan's simple mind assumed that the Oracle was being deliberately evasive, and he felt exasperated; but he also knew that he should persevere. Annie would be displeased if he didn't. He realised that time was the key, and remembered what Annie had said about a prophecy. He was about to change the tense and use 'will,' but suddenly understood.

"Does Atlantis exist?" he asked.

"Yes."

"Where?"

"At a point that you would call the future. The priest of Sais is a seer. Solon misunderstands. Plato misunderstands"

Brendan had actually wanted to know the geographical location, but persevered on the Oracle's track.

"How far into the future?"

"I do not recognise your concept of time. What was, is; what will be, is. Everything is."

"I understand that; thank you. Can you tell me where in the world Atlantis is situated?"

"Eveywhere."

"What happens?"

"Greed is great and machines are too powerful. The value system collapses. Nature aids in its destruction. All life suffers. That is all."

The Oracle was still and silent. Only the crackling remained. It was apparent that the audience was over.

"Thank you," he said.

The shrouded head appeared to nod, and then turned to Annie.

"You wish to enter the world apart. That is your right, lady; you have no need of my consent or my assistance. But payment is required for the human."

Annie removed one of the charms from her anklet, and held it out.

"I offer silver from the island of Hibernia," she said.

A hand was extended from the cowl, a surprisingly young hand it seemed to Brendan. The head nodded again as the charm was placed in its upturned palm, and then the figure faded. The rock wall of the recess faded too, leaving an aperture with a clear view of a verdant landscape beyond.

The three travellers stepped through it and onto a wide ledge of dark grey rock. It gleamed, as though made of ageing silver, and beyond it lay a drop of dizzying depth. Growing along the leading edge were small, twisted trees, like dwarf monkey puzzle trees; and beyond them Brendan could see a massive waterfall. A wide river curving round from his right disgorged its cargo over a cataract of enormous proportions. He estimated its width at several hundred feet, and the frothing white water fell several hundred more, roaring as it went, into a body of grey-blue water.

It looked at first like a lake, but he saw that there was an opening at the far end leading to a sea of the same colour. The view was partially obscured by endless clouds of mist drifting aimlessly off the falling water. He felt the dampness in the air around him, but it was nothing like the cloying, dreary dampness of the Hungry Ghost Realm. This was fresh and energising.

The land to the left of the inlet was coloured the most vivid green, the luxuriant expression of woodland canopies and the grassy spaces between them. The ledge gave way to a gently sloping path leading down to it, and that was the direction Rabbit was taking.

"She's only been here once before," said Annie, "but she never forgets a direction. We'll accompany her, shall we?"

They followed the pebble track, and soon the roar of the waterfall faded to a distant murmur as they passed into a wood lining the slope that ran down to the inlet. The twisted trees gave way to broader, taller ones of more regular shape. A sweet smell of vigorous growth filled the air. The sense of life and abundance came close to matching that of Eden, and Brendan saw patches of familiar woodland flowers as they entered a clearing. There was no sun, and so the light was even. A comforting temperance suffused the bright, still air.

Brendan felt that he was in another version of paradise. Annie checked his reverie.

"There are beings here," she said. "No doubt a few will reveal themselves, although most are shy, especially since it's been so long since they saw a human."

"The Oracle said time doesn't exist."

"Not to her, it doesn't. She was speaking cosmically. But the beings here have time as you do; only they live longer – very much longer."

Brendan looked around, expecting faces to peer at him from behind the tree trunks. At first he saw nothing, and then he noticed that one of the trees had a face of its own, apparently protruding from the gnarled trunk. It stretched out further as he watched, and then a body appeared below it until a figure stepped out and stood before them.

It was a naked woman, of that there was no doubt; and yet she was evidently not human. She appeared to be a young adult, but she had no trace of hair. Her skin was almost pure white, as though it had never seen the sun, and her eyes were sharp and dark. They carried a questioning expression, emphasised by the tilt of her head and the pouting set of her mouth. She stood motionless. So did Brendan as he stared back at her. He saw the same phenomenon repeated with two other trees in the vicinity, and the two figures walked slowly to join their companion. They were almost identical and stood in a line, regarding Brendan quizzically. He found his voice.

"Who are they?" he asked quietly.

"You've heard of Eurydice, no doubt. These are her kin. They're tree nymphs."

"They're beautiful."

"Orpheus thought so, too."

The three women nodded briefly to Annie, and then spoke to her in a language he didn't understand. She answered them and a brief conversation ensued. Their gaze returned to Brendan.

"What did they say?"

"Not a lot. They're just curious about you. They wanted to know where you're from, why you're dressed so strangely, and whether you're a warrior. These girls are old enough to remember the Trojan War. I told them you're a traveller from a distant land, and that you find them beautiful. That's why they're smiling – see? They asked whether you might want to stay here and marry them. Humans are regarded as a bit of a good catch in this place. It's just the rarity value; don't get too excited. I told them you had pressing business back home and wouldn't be able to accept their generous offer."

Brendan felt both flattered and embarrassed as he returned the women's gaze with a smile of his own. They giggled to each other and started to walk uncertainly towards him.

"Oh dear! What do I do now?" he asked Annie.

"You won't have to do anything. Hear that sound?"

He strained his ears, but could detect nothing for a few seconds. The nymphs had obviously heard it though. They turned in alarm before fading into white mist and floating back to the trees. The sound of hooves started quietly at first, but gained in volume rapidly. It was coming from the direction of a dense patch of woodland facing them, and Brendan's fascination was tinged with trepidation as the noise grew louder. The ground began to shake, and then three figures crashed out of the trees and into the space between them.

"Centaurs! I don't believe it," he gasped.

"Yes, Centaurs," replied Annie quietly, an ominous tone colouring her usual easy confidence. "Show them deference; they can be dangerous. They're strong, arrogant, and confident in their position as superior beings. There should be no problem as long as you're with me."

"Do they know you, then?"

"Of course. They don't like me, but that's their problem. They know my position and my power."

Brendan regarded the foremost of the creatures now walking towards them. The body of a powerful, white, sixteen hand horse approached to within a few yards. Rising from its shoulders was a sturdy, heavily muscled man's torso carrying a bow in one hand. He looked up at the creature's face in awe. A bearded, dark-skinned countenance looked back at him with haughty eyes that seemed to revel in the prospect of confrontation. Brendan found the sight intimidating in the extreme, but fascination kept his eyes fixed on the creature's face.

"Don't stare at him, Brendan," said Annie firmly. "You're challenging him. Look away and bow."

Brendan averted his eyes immediately and dipped his head in the direction of the centaur. He detected no response, and realised he would have to follow further proceedings through his peripheral vision. Thus, he saw that the creature shifted its position to face Annie. He saw it offer a deep bow in her direction, which she returned more lightly. They began to speak, again in a language unfamiliar to him. The conversation went on for several minutes, and then the three centaurs moved away a short space to commune among themselves.

Their voices became raised. It seemed that one of their number was unhappy about something, but was losing ground to the other two, including the leader. Eventually they trotted away, but the belligerent one turned to look in their direction as they were about to re-enter the wood. It was a pointed stare and looked menacing, and then the creature turned again and followed its companions. Brendan felt nervous.

"What was that all about?"

"The leader is their most powerful warrior, but he's old enough and wise enough to know who I am. One of the younger ones wanted to kill you. He said that humans have no right here; that you are trespassing on their land. The leader wouldn't allow it, of course, since you're my guest. That was inevitable. You were never in any danger."

Annie's assurance did not entirely convince Brendan. As beautiful and wholesome as this place undoubtedly was, it was no Eden. He felt fearful. The centaurs had been bigger and more powerful than any picture he had ever imagined from his reading of Greek mythology. This was a menacing place and he felt anxious to leave. Annie's presence went some way to reassure him, but he was still nervous. He said nothing. Annie suggested they walk along the narrow strip of land separating the wood from the shore of the inlet that was now close by. There was someone she needed to pay her respects to, she said, and she assumed Brendan would prefer to avoid the shorter route through the wood itself. He preferred not to proceed in that direction at all, but agreed reluctantly.

Rabbit had kept out of sight during the incident. She ambled alongside them as they began to stroll along the sea shore but she seemed nervous, looking constantly in the direction of the trees and twitching her nose as she sniffed the air. They had only walked a couple of hundred yards when she stopped suddenly. So did Annie. They both looked in the same direction. Almost immediately, the belligerent centaur crashed through the undergrowth fringing the woodland margin. In no more time that it took Brendan's fear to rise sharply, it removed an arrow from the quiver, fitted it, drew back, and fired at him. Brendan turned away and dropped to the ground, expecting a searing pain to engulf his body at any second. He felt nothing, but he heard a muffled thump. He looked back to see Rabbit lying a few feet in front of him, the arrow impaling her fragile form from one side to the other. It was obvious that she had leapt to intercept the missile and save his life. The centaur stood motionless in front of the trees, grinning arrogantly.

Brendan's shock kept his grief at bay for several mute seconds, during which time his emotions hung in some formless void of unreality and incomprehension. His fear of the centaur disappeared as his anguished eyes regarded the playful, inquisitive and eminently lovable Rabbit, now lying lifeless in front of him. She had become his friend, and now she had sacrificed her life to save his. He crawled over to her still form and his grief broke.

"Oh, no. Oh God, no," he stammered as the horror came fully home to him, and a terrible urge to sob began to well in his knotted throat.

Anger flared quickly, pushing his grief aside, and a manic desire for revenge came with it. He looked at the centaur again, his eyes filled with hate and his mind consumed with the will to send the creature tumbling backwards, as he had done to that hideous monstrosity in the Hungry Ghost Realm. Where was that power now? How could he use it to hurt the vile, arrogant being that had killed his friend? He wanted to hurt it; he wanted to visit unimaginable pain on it; he wanted to kill it.

The centaur stood its ground and sneered back at him. It took another arrow from the quiver, and twirled the missile between its fingers mockingly. Brendan leapt to his feet and looked around for something he could use as a weapon.

"Steady, Brendan," said Annie calmly. "Do nothing; there's no need."

Brendan looked at her, incredulous at her apparent lack of concern. He knelt close to Rabbit's pitiful body again, and was about to take her lifeless form into his arms when Annie knelt down and removed the arrow. She stood up, pointed the arrow at the assailant, and then threw it high into the air over the water. It flew straight and swift, and carried much further than it would from a bow, before plunging into the boiling foam beneath the cataract. Brendan sensed it was Annie's demonstration of superior power. Turning back to the centaur, she directed a menacing finger and said something in his language. Her voice was low, dark and supremely venomous.

The creature looked dismissive, and was turning to walk away when its two companions crashed urgently out of the wood. The leader assessed the scene quickly. Harsh words were exchanged and a brief struggle ensued. The younger centaur was soon overcome and held firmly. The leader nodded to Annie, and then galloped away with the transgressor.

"It's OK, Bren. You didn't really think the mother of all rabbits could die, did you, just from a bit of an arrow?"

Brendan's mind went into a state of shock as he looked to see Rabbit sitting perkily in front of him, her ears cocked high and a nonchalant look on her face. He felt numb; his mind was spinning and refusing to settle on an explanation. It didn't matter; he swept Rabbit into his arms and cradled her to his neck. He looked up at Annie, who seemed quite unmoved.

"Come on," she said firmly. "You need to learn to control your emotions, Brendan. We have business to finish."

Brendan had trouble speaking as he sought to keep pace with Annie, now striding swiftly and with a look of burning anger flooding her eyes. The emotional turmoil of the last few minutes was matched by the shock he felt at seeing her in this mood. He spluttered a question.

"What was that all about? Did Rabbit really save my life?"

"Yes, but if she hadn't I would have caught the arrow."

"So why did she lie still like that?"

"Just a temporary paralysis."

Brendan wanted to know more. He sensed vengeance in the air, and his return to something approaching equilibrium had cooled his own wish for something he had never really believed in.

"What was all that with the arrow and the pointing? What did you say to him?"

"I condemned him to death by drowning. He will die tomorrow."

"Whoa, steady on. That's a bit extreme, isn't it?"

"No. It's the way things work at this level. He knew you were under my protection, and yet he tried to kill you. I won't tolerate that. Tomorrow he will be wading through the shallows of one of the small rivers that flow over the falls. My sisters will lead him there, and they already have my instructions as to how to proceed. The rocks beneath his hooves will slip away and he will stumble. The river will sweep him over the falls and he will drown, exactly where the arrow fell into the sea."

"It still seems a bit extreme. I mean, there's no harm done."

"It isn't so extreme. Centaurs are reborn too, you know. Think of it as a lesson."

Brendan fell silent for a while, struggling with his conscience. He had never believed in capital punishment. An eye for an eye had always seemed wrong and backward to him. He wanted to oppose Annie's action; and yet he felt he had no right to interfere. Annie seemed to understand his difficulty.

"Your attitude is right as far as humans are concerned, Brendan," she said. "The prophet Jesus instructed people to turn the other cheek, partly because it is an act of compassion, but mainly because he knew that vengeance simply transfers the karmic debt to the reverse aggressor. You have spiritual growth to attain. I don't, and neither do centaurs Once a centaur, always a centaur. Don't concern yourself."

Brendan felt there was nothing more he could say on the matter and went silent again. They were entering a track that led into the wood before he asked another question.

"Who are we going to see?"

"The lord of the forest. He and I share a similar position. I was going to pay my respects anyway, but now there is an adjudication to be dealt with. It would be impolite not to gain his approval, although the outcome is a formality."

They walked on until they entered a circular clearing, much like the one in which he had seen the fairies dance in Ireland. This was bigger, though, and surrounded by silver birch trees taller than any Brendan had ever seen. Their massive crowns covered the circle with a grey-green canopy, and their sturdy silver trunks had the appearance of columns in an ancient temple. A single large rock stood in the middle, and next to it stood the three centaurs. The one in the centre was bound and looked apprehensive. The leader turned to Annie and nodded again. She returned it politely, and then they all directed an expectant gaze at a dark space between two trees on the far side.

Brendan felt the ground shake again, more evenly this time, as if made by a human treading on a sprung floor. What appeared from the gap was no human, but a massive figure walking on the hind legs of a goat. The torso and head were those of a man, similar to the centaurs but with two differences. This figure dwarfed them in its show of strength and power, and its head sported two curved horns. A hint of green mist hung about its form as it sat on the rock and beckoned Annie to come forth. Two satyrs held station a pace behind him.

"Stay here," instructed Annie. "Don't move and don't stare at him."

She walked towards the figure and stopped next to the leader of the centaurs, who was bowing deeply. Annie half bowed and the figure returned it in like fashion. She spoke, again in a strange language. The centaur spoke too, and then the great figure's eyes turned to the transgressor and delivered what appeared to be a short lecture. The leader bowed again, and all three galloped away. Annie conversed with the figure for a short while. The atmosphere between them appeared convivial and there were no parting formalities when they each retired to opposite sides of the circle. As soon as she reached Brendan she took his arm and led him quickly away.

"That's that," she said triumphantly. "Let's be making our way to the water. I want to get back to familiar territory."

Brendan remained incredulous at what he had just witnessed.

"I suppose it would be too much to hope that what I just saw was the Great God Pan?"

"No, it wouldn't. That was Pan all right; but there you go with that 'god' word again. He's the spirit of the woods and groves. I look after the water and the harvest. That's all."

"So what was the formal audience about?"

"I told him what happened, and the centaur's leader could do no other than confirm it. I demanded my right to mete out justice on my terms, and Pan agreed. It's settled."

There was no more talk as they walked to the lake. Brendan was coming to terms with what he saw as the harsh side of Annie, and she appeared to be allowing him the time. They remained silent for a while when they reached the water's edge and sat on a rock. Rabbit stayed apart, apparently avoiding the tinge of acrimony that she obviously felt. Brendan eventually settled into a philosophical frame of mind, and accepted that the nature of reality and the machinery of the more rarefied realms were beyond his capacity to judge. He looked pointedly at Annie, and she returned his gaze.

"Are you back with me?" she asked.

Brendan nodded, half apologetically.

"Where are we off to next?" he asked.

"To another place where the dead go," she answered. "Only, like everything else, it isn't so much a place as a state of mind. And don't look so alarmed. This one is very different from the other. You might even recognise it."

Despite Annie's relaxed attitude, Brendan felt alarmed. His one experience of being in a place where the dead go had been mentally devastating. Annie's assurances helped, but only so far. She had demonstrated that she had sufficient faith in his ability to come through that one, and he had gained a good deal of faith in her ability to know him well enough not to force him into anything he couldn't deal with. Nevertheless, it had been a singularly horrific experience and one he never wanted to repeat – even in a diluted form.

He looked at her questioningly for a few seconds. She and Rabbit returned his gaze, and then Annie's eyes turned slightly to look over his left shoulder. In the same instant, Rabbit hung her head and turned her back to him. He heard a noise behind him, and began to turn round. And then he caught a brief glimpse of something large and dark coming towards his head. In the short time he had to attempt recognition, it looked like the outstretched paw of a massive bear. He had no time to duck. His head resounded with an almighty shockwave and ear-splitting bang. The view dissolved instantly into a mess of blackness and searing flashes for a second, and then his senses switched off.

The Between

When they returned he found himself sitting with his back propped against a tree trunk. The first thing he saw was Rabbit's face, peering with evident concern into his. She was standing on his lap with her front paws pressed against his chest.

"It didn't hurt, did it Bren?" she asked.

Brendan felt dazed and shook his head. He wasn't sure exactly what Rabbit was talking about. He had a vague recollection of something hitting his head, but that was all. He remembered Annie talking of them going to another land of the dead, but nothing afterwards.

He saw Annie sitting a few yards away, regarding him with no more than passing concern. She had changed again. Her face now had the appearance of a beautiful, mature woman; and yet there were no wrinkles of blemishes that would normally betray advancing years. Her skin was as clear as the finest alabaster, and almost as white. Her dark blue eyes were large and luminous, and projected great wisdom as well as beauty. Jet black hair hung freely over her shoulders, and the shimmering white gown she was wearing seemed to be embroidered with pulsating forms that had the appearance of blood red flowers, golden ears of corn and spear-shaped green leaves. Winding around and between them was a ribbon of blue, like a river running through and nurturing a glorious landscape.

"Next stage?" he asked weakly.

"Final stage. How do you feel?"

"A bit dazed, but OK, I suppose. What happened back there? What hit me, and how did we get here? Whatever it was, I seem to be suffering a bout of amnesia."

"I'll explain later. Let's see if you can stand up."

He did so and found his physical faculties unhurt and fully functional. Annie moved towards him, the elegance of her walk and the straightness of her bearing seeming to suggest a glide, rather than a walk. Now she looked truly like a goddess. As she came close, Brendan saw that she was still the same height as him. Their eyes still met on equal terms. He felt profoundly gratified that she should choose to appear that way.

"What do you think of the view?" she asked.

Brendan looked around enthusiastically. They were at the edge of a wood, which lay behind them. A track ran out of it to his left, and passed a few feet away. It continued down a gentle, grassy slope and ran alongside a narrow lake lined with marble columns. At the end of the lake stood an elegant white building, also apparently made of marble, and having its own columnar structure redolent of the classical world. Two groups of people were passing along the road and entering it.

"So is this the place where the dead go," he asked.

"It is," said Annie, "but it isn't quite how it looks. I told you before that you can largely create your own reality when you die. Everybody does that until they're ready to move forward. Until then, they see who and what they want to see, or whatever their state of mind conditions them to see. But there needs to be a place of communal awareness so that individuals can go through the process of rest, evaluation, and preparation. That process involves a degree of interaction with other connected spirits. Often they need to be reborn in such a way as to be able to play out carefully defined roles in each other's lives. Like everything else below consciousness, this place is just another illusion; but it's as real to the people here as any place on earth. They see different things on the way to it, and they each see the building slightly differently. Some might see it coloured silver, some gold, some brick red - it all depends on the culture they've become accustomed to. You see it as white marble because you're from a culture that values the cool elegance and advanced philosophy of the classical tradition."

"Right. Interesting. So, does everybody come here?"

"Pretty much, all except the ones you saw in the Hungry Ghost Realm, and those who've reached such a state of enlightenment that they can come off the primary wheel and onto a more advanced one."

"That building looks a bit small to accommodate all the millions of souls who are between lives. All part of the illusion, I suppose."

"Of course. This place isn't three dimensional; it only looks that way."

"And I'll bet the same applies to time."

"Exactly."

Brendan looked beyond the columns and the building to the wider landscape. The woodland margin behind him stretched as far as he could see both ways. The vista in all other directions comprised a flat, green plain - grassland he assumed. The sky was uniformly blue, and yet there was no sun. There were no shadows either, but the view was bright and richly coloured, as it would be in high sunshine. Annie interrupted his study.

"We'll go and take a closer look shortly, but first I want you to tell me a story."

"A story? Why? What sort of a story?"

"A true story. The story of your relationship with Charlotte Stevens."

Brendan looked askance. He hadn't seen Charlotte Stevens for at least seven years.

"Good heavens! Where did you dredge her up from? What do you know about Charlie Stevens?"

"Never mind. Just tell me the story."

Brendan frowned. He was at a loss to know what on earth she could have to do with anything. But Annie was in charge here. If she insisted on hearing the story, no doubt she had a reason and he supposed he'd better tell it. He sat down by the tree again, and Rabbit came ambling up to recline by his leg.

"Go on, Bren, tell us the story. I like stories, and I don't know anything at all about Charlotte Stevens. Is it happy or sad?"

"Neither, really. It depressed the hell out of me at the time, but I got over it."

"Did you?" interposed Annie.

"Did I what?"

"Get over it."

"Yes, of course," he replied with a sharp frown. "At least... OK, she dragged me up the ladder of mad infatuation until I gave my heart to her, and then she dropped me like something you pick out of the gutter and suddenly realise what it is! It hurt. That's life."

He stopped when he realised that making such a statement to Annie was at least superfluous, if not presumptuous. He was heartened to see that her expression was unchanged.

"Go on, then," she continued, "let's hear the details."

Brendan frowned briefly at her, and then composed his thoughts. The dizziness had worn off and he was fully in command of his brain again, although he still couldn't remember a thing about how he'd got there. He supposed the memory would return in its own time.

"All right, here goes. I first met Charlie Stevens when I was working at a professional theatre. I worked front of house, but I had to go backstage on one occasion to meet somebody. I was sitting on a bench when the most stunning vision of loveliness came out of the rehearsal room. She was slim, elegant and exceedingly pretty. She had the grace of a dancer about her. What I most noticed, though, was her hair. It was very long, straight and lustrous, and was that version of red that looks like old gold. She turned to look at me and smiled. My breathing was arrested for a moment, and – silly cliché though it is - time really did seem to stand still. In what could have been no more than a couple of seconds, I picked up a hell of a lot of detail.

"Her skin matched her red hair – pale, with a hint of freckles. Her mouth was small, and suggested an element of reticence or reserve in her nature; but her eyes sparkled like gem stones. My word, did they sparkle! They were emerald green, and had that almond shape that gives them the impression of smiling, whether the rest of the face matches or not. I later learned that she had an Irish mother, which probably accounted for it. The look was brief, and then she turned away and disappeared into the workshops. I felt there was something fragile about her - not weak, but vulnerable somehow.

"The experience took me aback for a few minutes, and then I dismissed her from my mind. I was in my mid forties at the time and guessed she was about twenty years younger than me. I didn't have the slightest thought that any sort of relationship might be in prospect. I did enquire about her, though, and was told she was a junior member of the design team.

"It was September, about a week before the opening of the first play of the season. There was a staff party planned, and I was invited. Who should turn up at about midnight, but the red haired vision? I was sitting alone in the kitchen, having a quiet drink. She came in and sat opposite me.

"'Hi,' she said. 'I'm Charlotte; my friends call me Charlie.'

"I'd had a few drinks, and the sight of her taking an active interest in me set my pulse racing. It was the sort of situation in which amorous feelings are easily aroused, I suppose, age difference or not. 'Hello; I'm Brendan,' was the best reply I could manage. 'I know,' she said. 'I asked somebody who the guy in the suit was.' I'd gone there straight from work, you understand.

"Well, what was I to make of it? I was unattached and easily given to the adrenalin rush of romance. She seemed to be coming onto me, and my first instinct was obviously to reciprocate. We moved into the living room where the music was playing, and started to dance. Her body language was pretty explicit; not indecently so, but there was no doubt in my mind that she was interested in being something more than just a colleague.

"I went home in a dream at four o'clock and had trouble getting to sleep. It felt like Christmas Eve does when you're a kid, and I couldn't wait for Father Christmas to climb down the chimney. The following day I was brought back to earth; I heard that she'd got a freelance design job fifty miles away, and that she would be gone for three months.

"The cold light of day brought the cold light of reason with it. I knew I was smitten, and I was no stranger to the feeling. I'd had several long term relationships with women and they'd all failed. I knew why; it was because I was an incurable Romantic, and that meant I was always seeking something better, something more perfect. I knew I wasn't likely to change and so, some years before, I'd taken the decision not to indulge in romance any more; too many people were getting hurt. I knew that my addiction to it was incurable, and the only way to address it was to abstain. I was flattered by Charlie's interest, but decide to leave it at that.

"And then, three months later, I got a Christmas card from her. It said she was back in the area, and had moved into a flat about a mile away. The fact that she'd bothered to tell me rekindled my sense of flattery and I gave into it. Stupid of me, I suppose, but we all have our weaknesses. She'd included her phone number, too, and so I rang it. We agreed to meet for a drink.

"She insisted on telling me all sots of negative things about herself. At first I was surprised, but then I realised it was a test of my staying power. The game was afoot, and I was in the mood for playing it. It was Christmas, after all.

"We started seeing each other regularly at the theatre. Sometimes we would watch a show together; sometimes we would just have a drink when she finished work. When there was a first or last night party planned, we went together. It seemed to me that we were becoming an item. But I was having doubts, and they were getting stronger. I remained painfully aware of my resolution not to have any more romantic liaisons, but the aroma of romance is the most powerful narcotic to a true Romantic. It's like putting a glass of malt scotch in front of someone trying to kick an alcohol addiction. I was being tested, and it was driving me insane.

"Nevertheless, we continued to see each other, and her body language was becoming ever more explicit. My past experiences still kept me reticent. She invited me to lunch at her flat a couple of times, and seemed bemused by the fact that I was nibbling, rather than engaging with the occasion. I knew why; it was because my head and my heart had become wild horses, each trying to pull me in the opposite direction. In short, I was in turmoil.

"Things came to a head on 15th March. I remember the date because it's the Ides of March; the day on which Julius Caesar was assassinated... Ha!

We watched the first night of Hamlet, but there was no party planned so we went back to my place when the bar closed.

"There was something odd about her mood that night; it felt as though she was building up to say something. We exchanged small talk for a while, and had a few more drinks. I mentioned that I'd always wanted to learn to waltz, and that seemed to catch her interest. She said she knew how to waltz, and would teach me. I put some suitable music on and we both stood up. The intimacy of having my arm around her waist tipped me over the edge. Strange as it might seem, I'd never done that before. I entered some heady, euphoric state and capitulated. I gave in completely. After three months of torment and indecision the matter was settled; my heart had won. It seemed the feeling was mutual, because we fell into each other's arms.

"Or did we? I don't know. Maybe it was only me who fell, because something strange happened. I seemed to go into a daze, and when I came out of it I was standing alone on the carpet. Charlie was sitting on the sofa, and I had no idea why. All I knew was that I felt a devastating sense of rejection. She asked me whether I wanted her to leave. I looked at the clock – it was 1 am – and said 'no.' I sat on the floor next to her legs and leant back against the sofa. I felt emotionally drained, but I was refusing to give in.

"And then I went into some strange state again – this 'daze' or whatever it was. I assume it must have been caused by the combination of alcohol and high emotion, I don't know. When I next looked at the clock, three hours had passed. I had no recollection of those three hours; it seemed we'd passed them in silence. Charlie was still sitting on the sofa, staring into space. I looked pointedly at her, hoping for a response. She declined to look back at first, and then she turned her eyes towards me. They told me all I needed to know, or I thought they did. There was an unaccustomed coldness and sadness there. It was over; I was wrong; Charlie and I weren't an item. She said she was going home, and I insisted on accompanying her. If it was over, at least I could still play the gentleman.

"It was a horrible walk. An earlier snowfall had frozen, and the footprints on the pavement had turned to cratered ice. I saw her to her door and walked back feeling wretched. There was a full moon, I remember; it seemed to be mocking me. I continued to feel wretched for about six weeks afterwards, and I never saw her during that period. I had no reason to go backstage, and she had no reason to come to the front. When I did eventually see her again I tried to make friends, but there was a barrier between us that never came down. She married an actor eventually, and started a family. And that was that."

"That wasn't that, though, was it?" said Annie.

"What do you mean?"

"You've been thinking about her nearly every day for the last seven years, and you dream about her frequently."

"How do you know that?"

"I'm not quite the stranger you think I am. I've been taking an interest in you for a while; it's why I decided to bring you on this journey. There's something about you, Brendan; something to do with advanced sensitivity and the need to know just what is going on with this thing you call life. A few humans catch my attention; you're one of them. I'm going to show you something. Let's walk back along this track a little way."

The three of them sauntered off into the wood. Rabbit wasn't scampering in her usual way; she seemed content enough, but she was hopping – dutifully it seemed – alongside Annie. Brendan had the impression that this place possessed some gravitas that made it unsuitable for play. Annie, on the other hand, had an elegance and grace about her that gave him a sense of total confidence in her. She looked perfectly at home and in control here.

They passed two groups of people, walking in the direction of the white building. Those in the lead looked quizzically between Brendan and Annie a few times, before continuing to talk to their charges. They reached a point where a side path lad off from the main one, and Annie turned onto it.

"This place is special," she said. "Few people have the honour of coming along here."

"Why? What's so special about it?"

"You'll find out."

They reached a point where a clear plot of ground lay to the right of the track. A pristine white balustrade stood a few paces away, and in the middle of it was the top of a set of steps.

"Walk down those steps and wait," said Annie.

"What, on my own?" asked Brendan.

"Yes."

"Why?"

"Because you won't need me down there. You'll be in the presence of a greater power than me. Rabbit and I will wait for you."

Brendan felt both apprehensive and excited; he'd been certain that Annie was the greatest power he would ever be likely to meet. He hesitated briefly, and looked at her. She nodded in the direction of the steps. He walked over to them and began the descent.

What he saw stretched out below him was a sunken garden, stretching far into the distance. Glittering marble paths enclosed random beds full of perfect, succulent growth. There was no withering here; everything was in the prime of vigorous life. Shrubs and trees laden with spring-green leaves sat easily with winding creepers and a profusion of flowering plants. Small, temple-like structures were placed comfortably here and there, and the air was heady with a plethora of exquisite scents.

He reached the bottom of the steps and remembered Annie's instruction to wait. There was a marble bench a few feet away, and so he sat on it and waited. He looked around for a while, and then stared ahead, marvelling at a vista that seemed endless, even though the balustrade had appeared to be only a dozen feet in length.

His vision began to undergo a change that he found disturbing. The periphery became cloudy, leaving only a narrow tunnel of view directly in front of him. He had become used to strange incidents, and realised soon enough that this was probably as it should be. Something walked into that tunnel, and stood facing him.

It consisted of two presences. One was a large, glowing form that defied description. What it lacked physically, however, was more than compensated for by an immense sense of peace, compassion and power that flowed from it. It was the power of motherhood; the essence of the feminine principle in what he could only surmise was its profoundest form. This, he had little doubt, was some emanation of the Divine Mother.

He felt an immense weakness take hold, and began to slip from the bench; but he was immediately lifted by a force that had no physical identity. A sense of great joy and love swept over him, and he turned his attention to the second figure which was apparently holding the hand of the Mother. She was entirely human in appearance: a little girl, maybe nine or ten years old – and she looked exactly like a childhood version of Charlotte Stevens. Her hair was shorter, but the colour of old gold was just as he remembered it, and those emerald eyes left him in no doubt. Her face expressed a hint of diffidence, questioning, suspicion even. She leaned into the side of the Mother, and then a voice broke the silence. It was a gentle, caring voice.

"This child is as lost and frightened as you were. You must love her unconditionally."

There followed a profound silence as Brendan and the child regarded one another. Time seemed suspended, neither quantifiable nor infinite; it simply ceased to exist. The image faded and normal vision returned to Brendan's eyes. It clouded again as water filled them. His whole being was washed with an array of emotions: awe, peace, love, bliss – and others that he couldn't begin to identify. He sat calm and alone for what seemed like a long time. He felt his strength return gradually, and decided he ought to be getting back to Annie and Rabbit. He stood up, took a last look at the garden which he felt so profoundly privileged to have seen, and climbed the steps. The track was empty, but he saw his two companions waiting at the far end. He walked back to them, and began to tremble violently.

"I'm sorry..." he stuttered, shaking his head.

Annie placed her hands on his shoulders.

"Sorry for what? You should have some understanding of the energy you've just been exposed to. If you'd been less spiritually advanced, I wouldn't have taken you there; it might have reduced you to a gibbering moron. And that was only the lighter end of the scale. Take your time."

Brendan looked into Annie's eyes, and saw there a hint of that energy. He wanted to hold her close, or rather be held by her. He knew it wasn't the time or place, and so he asked a question.

"The child looked exactly like Charlie Stevens. Does that mean she's dead?"

"No. What you saw was her higher self. Humans split when they take earthly bodies. Only the lower self goes through the human experience; the higher self stays here. And it's the higher self which appears in a way appropriate to its degree of spiritual growth. That's why I wanted you to see her. She was part of your own growth, and you hers. It's a connection that will continue in different forms in other lifetimes. Any romantic relationship on earth this time round would have been pointless. It was never meant to be. You moved on, didn't you, and met someone who was a kindred spirit – somebody you're still very close to?"

"I did, yes."

"There you are, then. That explains the business of Charlotte Stevens. You needn't fret about her any more. Are you ready to carry on and see what happens in the big white building?"

"Will you be coming with me this time?"

"No. This is something else you can do on your own. You'll find lots to distract you in there. Rabbit and I would only get in the way."

"So, what do I do?"

"Just walk down that road and enter by the first door you come to. There are no security guards or dogs. You won't get arrested or anything."

Brendan stood uncertainly for a few seconds.

"Are you sure everything will be OK?"

"Yes. Go on. When you want to come back, we'll be waiting for you by the wood. Take as long as you need. Time is an illusion, after all"

He turned and began the walk that would take him down to the lake. Before he got there, he stopped and turned round. Rabbit was standing upright on her hind paws, watching him. Annie waved. He waved back, and then carried on to walk alongside the water. In what seemed to be no more than a few seconds, he found himself standing in front of a line of massive Doric columns. Behind them, a large doorway stood open. It had no door, and there was nobody in sight either to bar his way or invite him in. He felt truly alone, but the only way to go was forward.

Further Between

Brendan moved nervously towards the doorway and looked inside. A long corridor stretched into the distance as far as the eye could see. His initial sense of amazement at this spatial improbability was soon tempered by the understanding that it was merely the workings of a three dimensional illusion. He took a few tentative steps and looked around.

The floor was made of light wood parquet blocks, polished to a modest shine and flawless in every respect. They were laid in a herringbone pattern, which he found attractive. That was the clue to it, of course. He liked light wood, and he liked herringbone. What he was seeing on the surface was what he was projecting there.

The wall to his right was constructed of blank, finely dressed limestone, interrupted every few feet by small recesses containing marble statues of ancient deities. At intervals of maybe twenty feet, the wall was supported by round-topped Norman arches made of the same pristine limestone. That was predictable, too; he liked Norman architecture. So was the medieval vaulted ceiling twelve feet above his head and decorated with exquisite paintings redolent of the Renaissance masters. The left hand wall was the same as the right, except that it had doorways placed regularly along its length. He began to walk, and peered into the first doorway he passed.

It appeared there was some sort of reception going on. A young black man was sitting on a chair looking highly distressed. He was dressed in simple, ragged clothes, and his whole body shivered with a speed that looked unnatural. There was a dark patch in the middle of his chest, and Brendan surmised that it was the site of a fatal wound. Several people stood around him, looking calm but concerned. An elderly woman knelt at his side talking quietly to him, her hands moving through the air and enclosing him in a soft, golden light which Brendan assumed was some sort of healing energy. He felt a wave of compassion for the young man whose whole being seemed to have been fractured by a terrible experience. The shivering slowed and the first hint of calm crept onto his face. The dark patch lightened, too, and the young man smiled weakly. He saw Brendan watching him, and nodded a greeting. Brendan lifted one hand, and then moved on.

The second doorway revealed the figure of a middle aged woman standing just inside the threshold. She stared questioningly at Brendan as he approached. She had the look of an Indian, and the sari she was wearing appeared to confirm it. Her look was kind, but became increasingly inquisitive as he got closer, and she spoke when he drew level.

"Why are you alone?"

Brendan became defensive; he felt like a trespasser and wondered how he would stand up to interrogation.

"Don't be alarmed," continued the woman. "Nobody is going to hurt you. If you're here you must belong here, and you will find only peace and kindness. There's no one to interrogate or judge you. But you look lost, and that cannot be. So I ask you again: why are you alone?"

"Shouldn't I be?"

"No, of course not. You should be with your guide."

"Oh, her, yes; she stayed outside."

"Why?"

"I don't know."

The woman looked mystified. "Who is your guide?" she asked. "What's her name?"

"I don't know. She didn't tell me her name."

The woman's expression changed. Her smile continued, but it became indulgent and one eyebrow lifted.

"You will soon learn that you cannot hide things here. We know an untruth immediately. Why don't you want to tell me her name?"

Brendan felt guilty and exposed; he decided he had no option but to capitulate and rely on complete openness.

"Sorry. You caught me off guard. Her name's Annie."

"Annie? Annie? I know no Annie, at least not on that level. Did you know her in life?"

"Yes, sort of. I'm not actually dead, you see. Annie is bringing me on a journey. She said I could have a look at this place."

The woman nodded even more indulgently, and her face carried the unmistakeable light of understanding.

"Well, I know you're telling me at least what you believe to be the truth, so it's obvious you're confused at the moment. That's perfectly normal with many new arrivals. What I don't understand is that it constitutes all the more reason for this 'Annie' to stay close to you. I can't think why she would let you walk in here alone. This is most irregular. No matter; there must be a reason and no harm can come to you. As my own charge hasn't arrived yet, let me take you to your group room."

Brendan felt irritated. He didn't want to be taken to his group room, whatever that might be, or anywhere else. Annie was the person who took him places; Annie was the one he trusted. If he was to be alone in this piece of the adventure, he wanted to explore freely without having strange women poking their noses into his business. But he realised soon enough that he was on highly unfamiliar territory here, and that complying with its rules was probably the best way to avoid complications. Nevertheless, he still felt moved to ask a question in the hope of stalling the woman's intent.

"How do you know where my group room is?"

"I don't, but there will be somebody you will recognise waiting for you. I can see that you're a fairly old soul, so I think I know which section you'll be in. We'll soon find it"

Brendan could think of no reason to refuse, and so they began to walk. He was shocked by the speed at which the doors were flashing by, even though the two of them appeared to be walking normally.

"Where did you spend your last life?" asked the woman, appearing to be taking a passing interest in him.

"How do you mean?"

"Well, which country was your home? Somewhere in Europe, I should say."

"I live in England, but you'd know that from my language, surely. You're talking the same one."

"Oh dear, you must have had a difficult passing. Do you really not remember even the basics? Let me give you a brief lesson, until your memory returns. The only language here is the one of universal communication. You are vocalising your statements and questions in what you think is English, because that's what you're used to. I only hear the statements and questions, not the language, and I reply with ones of my own. I'm not speaking English or any other human language. It just sounds like English to you. It will all come back to you once the trauma has eased away. There's no hurry, you can take as much time as you need; time isn't quite what you think it is here."

She chuckled at her last statement, and then the progress of the passing doors slowed to something approaching normal.

"I think you must be somewhere about here. Let's look for someone you recognise."

Brendan felt a pang of anxiety. He looked back along the corridor, wondering whether it was as straight as it had seemed. Becoming lost in any large building was bad enough, but this one wasn't even three dimensional. The need to be rescued was raising its cowardly head, but he pushed it away. It was part of the journey and Annie would never leave him stranded there. Would she? No, of course not. He engaged with the woman in looking for his 'group room.'

They passed several doors, each one having several people inside or someone waiting to welcome their charge. Brendan recognised none of them, but he stopped when they came to the only one so far that was completely empty. He felt an odd sense of recognition, and a warm impression of homely comfort. The woman read it immediately.

"Odd," she said with a frown. "The mystery deepens. Are you sure this is your room?"

"I don't know," replied Brendan. "How can I be sure? I've never seen this place before. At least..."

He stared open-mouthed as a figure emerged from a door on the far side of the room, and came anxiously towards him. He felt a mixture of confusion and delight as he recognised Jenny, a dear friend who had died prematurely of cancer a few years earlier. The look on her face carried both shock and concern.

"Brendan, what are you doing here? We didn't know you were coming. We've made no preparations. I felt your presence, but couldn't believe it; yet here you are."

She came up close and took both his hands in her own. She kissed him on the cheek, and then looked questioningly into his eyes. Brendan was unsure how to reply. The Indian woman was still standing beside him, and she had already decided that he must be "confused," so he looked at her in the hope that she would say something to put Jenny's mind at ease.

"Your friend is confused," she repeated obligingly. "His passing must have been highly traumatic, though how it wasn't known about and prepared for I really can't imagine. This is a most singular occurrence. Still, at least he's in the right place now, and I have to get back for my own new arrival. I'll leave him with you, shall I? No doubt it will all be explained eventually. Good luck my friend."

With that, she walked away, and disappeared almost in an instant. Brendan was now free to talk.

"It's the most incredible thing that's ever happened, Jen. For the last week or so, I've been taken on an incredible journey by a woman and a rabbit. Yes, I know it sounds weird, but it's true. I'm not quite sure who the woman is yet; she's gone through various changes of appearance from a little girl to a beautiful, mature woman. I'm fairly sure she's a Celtic goddess, but she hasn't confirmed it yet, at least not directly. I've seen fairies, wood nymphs, water sprites, centaurs; I've been taken to other worlds and other dimensions; and then she brought me here and – can you believe this – I saw Charlie Stevens as a little girl. Remember her – from the theatre? And now I'm supposed to have a look around this place to see what the afterlife's all about. I'm not dead, you see. I'm really not dead. Oh, and by the way, it's absolutely fabulous to see you. I always knew you and I had a connection, right from the first moment we met."

Jenny continued to look concerned.

"Charlie is in a group associated with ours," she said, "but she hasn't come over yet. If you saw her, it must have been her higher self."

"Yes, it was; that's what I was told. It was explained to me why our relationship didn't work out. All part of the game we play, right?"

"Right," said Jenny quietly. She appeared to be pondering how she should handle an unforeseen situation that had suddenly been placed under her control.

"Come and sit down, Brendan. Let's talk and I'll see whether I can get to the bottom of this."

Brendan felt irritated again. Jenny obviously didn't believe him, but he was happy to sit and talk to her. He had been very fond of Jenny, and they had sat and talked often.

"Tell me the last thing you remember before you came here," she began.

He told her about the Oracle and the land beyond, how he had met tree nymphs and centaurs, and even had an arrow shot at him.

"And before that?" she continued.

He told her how awful the Hungry Ghost Realm had been, and how profoundly it had affected him. Jenny looked particularly interested in that recollection, and shook her head.

"How on earth did you manage to end up there?" she said, seeming to be addressing the question to herself. "OK, she said eventually. "Forget all the events of this journey you've been on, and tell me: what's the last thing you remember on earth – before you began the journey."

He told her of the walk up the hill, and how he had encountered the farmer, the little girl and the rabbit. He recounted how it had all begun by being taken into a pool, before journeying across an ocean.

"Drowning?" mused Jenny. "Can't be, surely."

"Jenny, why don't you believe me? I keep telling you: *I'm not dead.* All this *happened*; it really did."

She took Brendan's hands into hers again and looked fondly into his eyes. This was the Jenny he remembered best. She had always been a caring, compassionate soul with time for anybody who needed her. It was why she had been a living legend among her friends and colleagues, and why her funeral service had been packed to capacity. It felt odd, remembering the funeral of somebody he was now talking to. Jenny was gathering her thoughts, and then continued.

"Brendan," she began hesitatingly, "there's no easy way to put this. I don't know where this confusion of yours comes from, because I sense no trauma in you. You seem perfectly relaxed to me, and so I'm going to give it to you straight. You *are* dead; you have to be. There's no way you could be here otherwise. Something odd is going on, I grant you. I've never known a situation when we weren't well prepared for somebody's arrival. But being dead is non-negotiable. You have to accept it, my old friend. Brendan Bradshaw had his life, as Jenny Baker did, but they've gone now; they've moved on. I don't know what we'll be to each other in the next life because we haven't discussed it yet. That's the problem with not being prepared. But dead you certainly are. That's a fact."

Brendan was doing his best to subdue the level of frustration that was rising in him. He was human, and so to him the journey with Annie was incredible; but he thought that Jenny would have a better understanding of such things. It seemed she didn't; she found it as unbelievable as any human would. He began his defence.

"Jenny, we were very fond of each other, weren't we? I don't think we ever quarrelled in the seven years I knew you. But I have to tell you now that you're wrong. This journey of mine isn't imagination. I'm not dead. If you don't believe me, come outside and meet the person who brought me here. She's waiting at the end of the track by the wood."

A look came over Jenny's face. Brendan was becoming a little tired of people looking at him indulgently. He stood up and began to pace the room in frustration, until a group of people appeared from the inner door. He caught his breath as he recognised his mother, his step father and his brother. They were all walking towards him with the same concerned expressions that seemed to be the standard greeting in this place. Nevertheless, he was astonished and overcome by their appearance. His mother hugged him tightly and he reciprocated. The moment temporarily shook his equilibrium and his belief in this situation or any other. The last time he had seen her, she had been lying dead in a hospital bed. He remembered her funeral, too. He regained his full composure when she spoke.

"We didn't know you were coming, Brendan. We would have greeted you properly. What happened?"

"Nothing happened. I'm not dead. It's a long story."

His mother looked questioningly at Jenny, as his brother slapped him firmly on the arm.

"It's good to see you, mate. Don't know what went wrong, but don't worry about it. It'll all be sorted out in rehab. Hey, what did you think of that trick I pulled on the MG car alarm, the night I died? It was Peter Bentley who showed me how to do that. Remember Peter? He was the one who came to collect me."

"Oh, it was noticed, all right. Everybody said they were sure it was you. I told them they were probably right."

Brendan realised he was becoming blasé about the whole situation. He knew it was borne of the frustration he felt at being unable to convince them. He heard a cough, and looked at his step father who was standing back from the others. The man had been eminently dislikeable. He had been an abusive martinet who had tried to instil many bad values in the young Brendan.

"Hello Brendan," he said, with a note of apology in his voice. "I hope you've forgiven the way I was to you. It was all role play, as I'm sure you must remember now – teaching each other lessons, and all that."

"I don't remember, no; but I worked it out for myself a good many years ago. I stopped feeling bitter; there are no hard feelings."

"Good man," he said, holding out his hand which Brendan shook.

Jenny had joined the group, and pulled Brendan's arm around her own.

"I think we'd better be getting you inside," she said, with that gentle, motherly tone he had always associated with her.

"To do what?"

"You really don't remember, do you? First there's rehab to get rid of any negative overhangs; then there's reflection counselling, where your life is discussed and evaluated; then we start the group sessions where we examine the reality models and plan the general road of our next lives. Now you're here, we only have one more member of the core group to come over. We can't finalise things 'til then, but we can be getting some groundwork done. We've already started."

Jenny began to move forward, but Brendan resisted. His fear of getting lost was coming to the fore again, and he didn't want to go through that door. It might separate him from Annie; he might be trapped here. He might actually die for real.

"Look, all of you. How can I make you believe me? I'm really not dead. I'm on a journey and have been brought here to see what happens between lives. Unconventional it might be – unprecedented even, I don't know - but it's true. Please, just come outside and meet the person – although she's hardly that, exactly – who brought me here. She'll explain everything."

His mother and step father shook their heads; his brother looked embarrassed, and seemed to scoff inwardly. Jenny looked at him with an intense but calm stare. He had rarely known her to be anything other than calm.

Wisdom, tolerance and understanding had always been her hallmarks. He pleaded with his eyes, and she reacted in her own, inimitable way.

"All right, there's no hurry to get started. Let's all go outside and meet this personage you keep telling us about. Maybe she'll clear up the mystery, eh?"

Brendan felt patronised, and the others looked uncertain, but they followed dutifully as he led the way out of the room. The walk back along the corridor was the same as before – the doorways flashing by at speed as the group walked normally. Soon they were at the outer door and Brendan felt the mightiest sense of relief as he saw the figures of Annie and Rabbit standing by the wood, just as they had been earlier.

"There," he said. "Told you. We'll soon get to the bottom of this."

He quickened his pace, leaving the others to fall behind as he hurried impatiently to what he saw as the arms of rescue. Annie looked imperious, gently welcoming, and very beautiful. Rabbit ran towards him and nuzzled his nose when he bent down to greet her.

"You've no idea how glad I am to see you," he spluttered to Annie. "Would you please explain to these people that I'm not dead and that I'll be leaving here with you and Rabbit?"

Annie said nothing, but Rabbit murmured something quietly that sounded like "It might not be so easy." Brendan heard Jenny's voice behind him

"Well?"

He turned to see all four looking expectantly at him. He turned around again to make sure that Annie was still standing there. He stretched out his arm and finger in her direction.

"Right, here she is," he said to the group. "Feel free to ask her what's going on."

It soon became clear from the set of their heads, the look in their eyes, and every other aspect of their appearance, that none of them could see Annie. Jenny confirmed it.

"There's nobody here, Brendan. Whoever you think you can see, she's obviously a part of some aberration going on in your mind. I don't know what; I've never encountered this before. But I really think you should start rehab without delay."

Brendan was speechless for a moment. He looked back at Annie, and found his voice.

"Annie, will you please talk to these people and show them you're really here?"

"Why?"

"Why!? Because they don't believe me, that's why!"

"So what?"

"They want to keep me here."

"That's all right. It doesn't matter what they want."

"Annie, please stop playing games. Why won't you show yourself to them?"

"Why should I?"

"Because I'm in peril here!"

"No, you're not. There is no peril here, and I'm not in the habit of revealing myself that easily to humans, be they on earth or here in the Between."

"But they won't believe I'm not dead."

"And they're right."

An icy hand clutched at Brendan's chest, mingled with a sense of disbelief. He stared at Annie, reluctant to ask the only question available to him. Annie never lied. Eventually, he asked it.

"Are you saying I really am dead?"

"Yes."

The hand strengthened its grip; it squeezed until his breathing grew shallow. He felt sick, confused, betrayed; and then he felt Jenny's hand laid gently on his arm.

"Come back now, Brendan. Everything will be OK once we get you proper help. You'll soon recognise where you are, and remember that you've been through it all many times before."

Brendan realised he had forgotten her presence momentarily, and that she must have heard one side of a very strange conversation. He also knew that Annie and Rabbit were still standing there, and that there was more he needed to know. There was something not right about this; the bottom had fallen out of every sense of certainty he thought he possessed. The experiences, the lessons, the wonderment of it all – everything had collapsed into a dull mist. The whole of his existence was suddenly in doubt.

"I want to stay here for a while," he replied as calmly as he could manage. "May I do that? I'll come in when I'm ready."

"Of course, if that's what you want. Nothing is disallowed here; you can come and go as you like, with one exception. You can't go back along that road. It doesn't lead anywhere; it's strictly a one way street. Once you reach this point, you can only go that way." She nodded her head in the direction of the building. "And I have to say that you shouldn't take too long about getting help. You'll continue to suffer until you do. We all love you, Brendan. We just want what's best for you."

With that, she and the others turned and walked away. Brendan watched them for a little while, and then turned back to Annie.

"So, are you real or just part of my fevered imagination?"

"I'm as real anybody else you'll ever meet."

"And what about all those places you took me to, and all the people we met. Were they real?"

"Same answer."

"So, what's going on? You didn't tell me I was going to die. When did I die? How?"

"You died when the bear I summoned killed you with a single blow of its paw. It seemed the kindest, quickest, least painful way to do it."

"You had me killed?"

"Yes. I had to in order for you to come here."

"So, what was the point of everything?"

"To give you a privileged view of things very few people ever get to see. That's what you agreed to embark upon."

"But the man at the pool assured me that I'd come out of it still with a human body."

"And so you shall."

"Oh, right, a *dead* body, you mean? What kind of trickery was that, for heaven's sake?"

"Brendan, stand up straight and look at me."

"Why?"

"Because you've made this mistake before. It was perfectly understandable the first time, but you shouldn't be doing it again. You learned to trust me; why have you stopped? How dare you accuse me of trickery? When have I ever tricked you, and why would I do such a thing?"

Brendan was shaking, but he looked deep into Annie's eyes. He saw a simmering heat there that would have cowed a braver man than him. He felt lost; he didn't know what to say, and so he said nothing.

"All right, Brendan. I understand that it must have been a shock for you, and maybe I'm not making proper allowance for human frailty. So let me ask you a question: do you trust me, or not?"

Something in the power of Annie's eyes brought that old feeling of connectedness back to him. In the midst of his agonising confusion, he sensed again that it was the one thing he could rely on.

"Yes."

"Good; so now I'll explain. Your friend Jenny was right. The path back there *is* a one way street; but we didn't come along that path, and we're not going back that way. How do we go anywhere?"

"By water."

"Right; and where do you see water?"

"The pool."

"Right again."

"So, we're going back?"

"Of course."

"And then I'll be alive again?"

"Not exactly. When we get back, your body will still be lying there. I asked the chief centaur to mount a guard over it. Then we'll set about bringing you back to life."

Brendan stood open mouthed and filled with a mixture of intense relief and astonishment.

"You can resurrect dead bodies?"

"Ordinarily, of course not. But this is different. Come on, let's walk. I'll tell you the rest on the way."

Rabbit kept close to Brendan's feet as they began to stroll towards the water. Annie rubbed his arm gently, just once. Her anger had dissipated; her eyes now carried a hint of compassion. She continued.

"Remember that I had to realign your energies to make them suitable for the land beyond? The body that was killed wasn't your native body, the energies were alien; and even though the life force is absent, the energies are still the basis of the physical structure. Once I bring those energies back to their proper level… well, wait and see what happens."

Brendan's trust in Annie exploded to new heights, and a familiar sense of shame came with it. He went silent until they reached the pool, and then a sudden thought struck him.

"If you knew I was going to have to die, why didn't you just let the centaur's arrow kill me?"

"That happened unexpectedly, and it would have been disastrous anyway. I had to prepare myself to take charge of your etheric body when the physical one was killed. If I hadn't done that, it would have gone off to the Between and entered via the track through the wood. If I hadn't got to you in time, there's no way I could have brought you back."

"And I really would have been dead."

"Yes. Ready?"

Rabbit leapt first, as usual; but Brendan was little more than a second behind her. As fascinating as this place was, getting out of it had become a major priority. He felt a brief pang of sorrow as he entered the water. It struck him that Jenny and the others would wonder where he had gone, and he felt guilty that he hadn't been able to say goodbye to them. He took refuge in the thought that he was leaving a mystery behind him as a legacy of his visit. That amused him briefly, but then he wondered whether such a mystery could exist here. Time, he had been told, had no meaning in the Between. Maybe in that pregnant but essentially empty moment when his heart finally declined to throb its next beat, he would return in the same instant as he had left. He would be able to walk confidently through the ever open doorway behind the columns and exclaim "OK, you win. Let's be off to rehab." That amused him, too.

Resurrection

Brendan was surprised at how different he felt during this latest trip through the water. There was no sense of holding his breath, nor any sensation of water flowing over him. He addressed the thought to Annie.

"That's because the water is physical, and you aren't at the moment. You're effectively a ghost. That's why it was so easy to get you to the Between and sit you up against that tree. Imagine what possibilities would open up if you could achieve that state at will. Some people can."

"So I've heard. Are you going to teach me?"

"No. It isn't my place to teach you tricks."

Brendan chuckled inwardly, and then another question struck him.

"What I don't understand, though, is how the water in the Between can be connected to the water in the Greek place. They're in different dimensions, surely."

"Why only ask that question now? It's been true of all the transitions we've made. Water is the fabric, for want of a better way of putting it, that connects all levels of existence. Why do you think seers, mystics and other practitioners in what you call magic have used it as the means of making contact with the gods – as you would have them called – and other realities? You know about the veneration in which pools were held among the ancient inhabitants of your own land, don't you?"

Brendan did indeed, and now it all seemed so obvious. As he relaxed into pondering the matter, he became suddenly anxious again. He remembered that he was dead, and that there was still some mysterious process to be gone through in order to reverse the fact. He felt disinclined to ask any more questions, and remained silent for the rest of the journey.

The trip was over surprisingly quickly, and soon they were walking out of the water. Brendan's ears were filled with the roar of the cataract plunging into the lake, and waves of conflicting emotions washed over him as he regarded the scene. He saw his own dead body stretched out peacefully, his own hands resting neatly on his own quiet chest as though he were some notable dignitary lying in state. He felt a stab of desolation and a poignant pang of his own mortality as he looked at the lifeless remains of Brendan Bradshaw. The sensation was mercifully brief; he overcame it quickly as he told himself that it was only a temporary state of affairs.

He wondered who had gone to the trouble of arranging his body like that. He felt a deep sense of gratitude to whoever it was, but what touched him more was the care and respect now being paid to it. Rabbit was sitting dutifully at its head, in the place he would expect a chief mourner to occupy. Two centaurs stood one on either side, protecting it from any attempt at disturbance. Four tree nymphs were in the process of carefully placing fresh green leaves over the whole of his recumbent form, and he assumed it was they who had lain the head on a pillow of multicoloured flowers. If that weren't enough to bring a lump to his throat, a fifth nymph was sitting cross-legged at his feet singing a song replete with mournful beauty.

"Do they know I'm going to be brought back to life?" he asked Annie.

"No, they don't need to. They think you were killed in a fight with a mighty animal, and that makes you a hero. Even the centaurs, as much as they dislike me, respect a warrior. Let them have their moment; there's no harm done."

They both stood and watched the poignant scene for some minutes, until the nymphs had completed their activities and the body lay covered in leaves.

"What happens now? When do you start rearranging my energies?" asked Brendan. For all that he trusted Annie, he was naturally anxious, and anxiety was giving way to a predictable impatience.

"I can't do that until we take the body back to your world. Realigning the energies here would be messy; the body would disappear. I could still see and work on it, but it would be in an environment that would make it difficult to function. I can't be sure your etheric form would be able to re-enter it. It's simpler and safer to take it back."

"So how do we get it back?"

"We carry it, or rather my sisters will. They're waiting behind you."

Brendan turned round to behold the sight of four water nymphs walking out of the lake. They were obviously the same as the ones that had accompanied his passage on the first journey, only this time they were not vague, flitting shapes. In form and stature they were the same as the tree nymphs, but their skins were pale silver and had a scaly appearance, as he had thought originally. And their hair was long and blonde, with an unmistakeably green tinge.

"They look like the way the merrow are described in Irish folklore," he said.

"Of course they do," replied Annie dismissively. "Now, don't interrupt for a few minutes. There is a potentially difficult situation to defuse."

Brendan heard an unearthly sound suddenly rise from the ranks of the tree nymphs. It was somewhere between a shriek and a wail, and sounded angry. Their faces carried a look of unbridled belligerence as they stared aggressively at the newcomers. It seemed that a battle was about to break out between the dryads and nyads for the body of Brendan Bradshaw. He found the prospect both exciting and unnerving, but permitted himself the brief indulgence of thinking it would make a fine tale to tell people around the dinner table! He noticed that Rabbit had vacated her station as chief mourner, and was ambling with Annie as she approached the apparently offended women. Annie's bearing conveyed the grace and authority appropriate to her status, and the nymphs fell quiet.

She began to talk to them in their own language, her posture erect but her voice low and measured. They answered her all at once, and began to make exaggerated gestures. Their voices rose and fell as Annie listened, and their postures betrayed extreme annoyance at the prospect of being relieved of the charge over which they had taken so much trouble. That was how it seemed to him, and he felt honoured. He turned to look at the water nymphs again. They were standing dutifully by the water's edge; but their eyes, too, revealed a readiness for battle, should it become necessary. Now he felt doubly honoured. He turned again and saw that Rabbit was watching him. He heard her giggle, and he smiled back.

There was no battle. After more conversation, the nymphs demurred and faded into five clouds of mist that returned to the trees. He assumed that Annie's authority, and maybe some diplomatic explanation, had carried the day without recourse to bloodshed. The centaurs bowed briefly to her, and galloped away.

Annie waved the water nymphs to come forward. They did so and, presumably under instruction to respect their arboreal cousins' efforts, removed the leaves one by one with due gravity. They laid them in two narrow piles either side of the body. Then they lifted it with apparent ease and carried it slowly to the water. Annie walked back to Brendan, while Rabbit went hopping off to the lake edge where the nyads were waiting for further instructions. Annie's face had that look he'd seen before – calm, controlled, superior, yet somehow motherly. She looked at least twenty years younger than him, and it was an odd contradiction that he found difficult to resolve.

"How does it feel, having two sets of beautiful young women prepared to go to war over you?" she asked, smiling.

"Unprecedented! What did you tell the tree nymphs?"

"That you were from another land far from here, and that it was only right that you should be taken back and buried with your ancestors. That didn't entirely convince them. They were finally won over when I explained that your fellow warriors would be denied the right to mourn you properly if I didn't."

"Oh dear, that wasn't entirely true."

"Yes it was. To them, you were dead; in fact, you *are* dead. I just didn't tell them that you're not going to stay dead. There was no need. And you're a warrior, too. You would have attacked that centaur who shot Rabbit with anything you could find if I hadn't prevented it, wouldn't you? Anyway, are you ready to say goodbye to the land beyond and re-engage with your physical shell?"

"Will it hurt?"

"It will be uncomfortable, but it won't actually hurt. Would you rather not?"

Brendan smiled graciously at Annie's sardonic humour. He shook his head and they walked into the water, preceded by the nymphs carrying his body. The surreal nature of the experience sent his mind into a whirl of uncertainty for a moment. He briefly wondered whether all this was just the product of a crazed imagination, a mental aberration brought on by some traumatic event, as Jenny and the others had so insisted must be the case. Or maybe it was an amazingly elaborate dream.

"Don't be silly, Bren."

It was Rabbit's voice again, and then he heard Annie's.

"And what do we keep telling you about the nature of reality? Just stay with me, and we'll finish this journey without mishap."

They sank beneath the blue-grey surface, and Brendan's mind went quiet again; but he felt the slightest twinge of consternation when he saw that the nymphs bearing his body were swimming swiftly ahead and fading into the murk. Soon they disappeared altogether. He knew there was no reason for concern, and was content to be pulled along by Annie's firm grip until his head rose above the surface of a more agitated sea.

He found himself following her onto the beach of a small cove surrounded by cliffs. His body was lying on the sand a few yards from the water's edge, and the nymphs were nowhere to be seen. He looked around and saw a familiar, heavy sea with cream-topped waves, rising and falling as proper seas should. A couple of what appeared to be small islands lay a little way off, and a mass of more substantial land rose up a few miles away. Hordes of seabirds wheeled and shrieked their incessant flight above his head, and several grey seals were watching him with apparent interest, their heads bobbing with the movement of the swell.

"Where are we?" he asked.

"On one of the many uninhabited islands beyond the Outer Hebrides. Nobody ever comes here, so we won't be disturbed."

"In my world, you mean?"

"Yes."

Annie studied the body for several minutes, and laid her hands on several points. Brendan remained quiet until she seemed to have completed her inspection.

"Is everything OK?" he asked nervously.

"Yes, everything's fine. It will take me a few minutes to fully prepare it, but all the organs are in working order. It won't be a problem. While I'm doing that, why don't you take advantage of your current state to see something you wouldn't normally be able to? We're off the continental shelf here, but the depth of water won't be a problem to you at the moment. Rabbit has something to show you."

"Do I?" asked Rabbit, looking between the two of them.

Some deep level of communication must have taken place between them, something that was beyond Brendan's means to hear, for Rabbit suddenly looked excited. And then he heard her voice again.

"Where?"

"In the bottom cave. She's with her young ones."

"Right, come on Bren. You'll like this."

She was already dashing towards the sea, and Annie was gesturing him to follow with a nod of her head. Brendan followed, and soon they were diving deep, deep, and deeper still. He was surprised that he could see clearly every detail of the dark grey rock face as they followed its sloping form down into the abyss.

"You're a ghost, Bren. Ghosts don't need light. And the fact that you're a ghost means she won't see you, so she won't be frightened away."

"Who won't?"

"You'll see."

Still they dived deeper, ever deeper. Brendan felt no physical sensation, but the very thought of such an astonishingly swift descent made him feel dizzy. Eventually the sea bed came into view, and he saw the dark mass of a large cave entrance at the base of the sunken mountain. Briefly, he was reminded of the Hungry Ghost Realm, and also the portentous patch on the man's chest in the Between. He felt uncertain for a moment, but Rabbit was rushing into the cave and he was happy to go with her.

They swam through a tunnel of regular dimensions for a little way, and then passed into a cavern of giant proportions. Brendan would have held his breath, if he'd had any breath to hold, for this was far more impressive than even the greatest cathedral. This was nature's construction at its most awe inspiring. He had been in many caves in his life, and had often found their grandeur impressive. They were mere babies; this was the grandfather of them all.

"There she is," said Rabbit pointing downwards. "Isn't she beautiful?"

Brendan looked down, and for the second time in a matter of minutes, felt the pointless need to take a sharp breath. There, resting on a ledge twenty or thirty feet below them, was a giant creature. He had seen pictures of it, and read of the speculation surrounding it. The humped body, the long, slender neck, the small head, the four great flippers, and the flattened tail; this was legend made manifest. Two smaller versions of the great body rested beside her, one on each side, and the visitors swam down to take a closer look. It was her massive eye that held Brendan fascinated. It was alert, but gentle as her offspring slumbered quietly beside her.

"She doesn't know we're here," said Rabbit. "Bet no human has ever seen her like this. Aren't you glad I brought you?"

Brendan said nothing; mere words would have been superfluous. This was more than special, and he hung there feeling only a massive sense of privilege and great gratitude for the circumstances that had brought him to her side. He was eventually moved to ask a question, but was interrupted when the mother stirred and the babies woke. She rose slowly in the water, and the young ones rose with her. A beat of her flippers propelled her forward, and soon she was heading into the tunnel. Rabbit and Brendan followed until they were back in the depths of the western ocean. She increased her speed there, and then the sea was empty again.

"That was incredible," he murmured.

"You bet! Don't see that every day, do you? I think we'd better be getting back, though. Boss lady is probably ready for you by now."

They began a rapid ascent, and that was when the physical discomfort began. His midriff felt bloated fit to burst, a vice closed around his chest, his head seemed to be swelling, and he felt hot, sick and dizzy. He thought he was sinking back into the depths, and the unreasonable notion swept over him that he was about to drown. Panic set in immediately, but then everything changed. He shot upwards, and the grey of the water was replaced by flashing, multi-coloured lights. His dizziness increased until his mind let go and darkness descended. All was still, and he opened his eyes. He saw white clouds scudding fitfully across a blue sky, and then the faces of Annie and Rabbit leaned over him and filled his view.

"Good, said Annie. That wasn't so difficult. Try sitting up slowly."

He pushed himself up with some difficulty, and looked around for his body. It wasn't there. He was back in it.

"There you are, alive and in fine fettle, but you'll need to rest for a few minutes. Your various parts have got to get used to working again. Here, drink this."

She passed him a large conch shell, filled to the brim with a colourless liquid.

"Where did you get this?" he asked.

"It's fresh water, Brendan. I have a way with water; haven't you noticed?"

She moved behind him, and he felt himself being lifted effortlessly until his back was resting against a rock. The water tasted good, and he began to feel stronger. Annie took up a cross-legged position facing him, and Rabbit climbed into her lap and dozed.

"What did you think of our friend in the cave?" she asked.

"Truly amazing," he replied humbly. "Was she who I think she was?"

"If you mean does she sometimes swim up the Great Glen and take the air in Loch Ness, yes. Many people have seen her, but none the way you did."

Brendan regarded Annie's elegant posture. She had sat facing him like that earlier in the journey, but she had looked like an ordinary little girl then. This was very different; apart from her greater physical maturity, he fancied he could see an aura of subtle luminescence surrounding her. He wondered whether it was really there, or a figment of his imagination.

"Your eye is becoming attuned to subtler forms of energy," she said, and then she went silent again.

She remained still, and continued to hold his attention with her eyes. They seemed to be growing ever more powerful, beautiful, gracious and full of knowledge. Any lingering doubt he had entertained concerning her identity was all but gone. Whatever force they emanated, it had its origin in a realm far from the world of mortal man; and it could only be a higher realm, he assumed. And some unspoken meaning was there, crossing the space incessantly between them. It was telling him that this journey was finite.

He felt an immense sadness well up. The journey had been beautiful and uplifting at times; at others it had been difficult, depressing, and even painful. As such, it had been a microcosm of life itself, but in a manner so extraordinary that he knew nothing in what was left of his life would ever come within a million miles of matching it. The thought of it having to end filled him with an aching sense of deep desolation.

But maybe the ending of the journey wasn't the only root of his feeling. He continued to look directly into Annie's eyes, and she continued to look steadfastly back; and yet the look was anything but disinterested. Her features betrayed no obvious trace of emotion, but her eyes projected layer upon layer of subtle statements that were beyond his means to understand. He declined to attempt comprehension. All he could know was that he was held in thrall to them. Annie broke the spell.

"Try to stand, let's see how strong you are."

He stood up, feeling a little groggy at first but soon gaining a reasonable grasp of his physical equilibrium. He strolled to the water's edge and back. Annie made no attempt to support him, as he knew she wouldn't. She had taken his life away, and she had returned it unharmed. The mere matter of walking was up to him.

"I feel fine," he said confidently.

"You are fine," she said. "You're stronger than you think."

And now her eyes seemed to show him something else, and this time he felt able to grasp the meaning. They seemed to be saying that she respected him. The corners of her mouth turned up almost imperceptibly.

"Are you ready to continue the journey?" she asked.

"You know I am."

"Yes, but you have to know it, too."

"You've taken me to the ends of the earth and beyond. Whenever you say it's time to go, I'm ready."

"Good."

"Oh, and Annie..."

"Yes?"

"Thank you."

The full smile she returned was the most captivating thing he had ever seen, on that world or any other. He felt some part of his being rush out of his chest like palpable matter. There was no doubting its reality; this was the stuff of divine consciousness, given free rein by a sudden burst of realisation that made him briefly mad with the joy of the infinite. Now he truly knew what the phrase "God is love" really meant. But its rein wasn't entirely free; it stopped a foot short of Annie's seemingly physical form, and returned as quickly as it had gone out. There was clearly one barrier that he was still not allowed to cross, and his spirit returned to the low side of normal.

"Where are we going next?" he asked.

"To show you how the pyramids were built."

"Ancient Egypt?"

"Not exactly. The time shift would be difficult for you at the moment, but there's a parallel version of it existing on a slower time line, the same as the Puritan village we went to. The same things are happening now as happened in your ancient Egypt nearly five thousand years ago. You say you're ready, so let's go."

Ancient Knowledge

It made a pleasant change, surfacing in a wide, slow flowing river instead of the usual lake or sea. Despite having the protection of Annie's doughy elixir against climatic extremes, Brendan still felt the heat of the noon sun as he waded between the profusion of reeds lining the riverbank. He regarded them with fascination, for he knew they were the fabled bulrushes of the biblical story of Moses. Comfortable memories of brightly coloured picture books came back to him. The Children's Book of Bible Stories – or a book with some such title – had been a source of great delight in those halcyon days of childhood, when his world was simple, optimistic and painted almost wholly in primary colours.

He stood for a while, thigh-deep in the tepid water, watching with rapt attention as their heads swayed serenely in the gentle breeze. He saw nature's music being played out there. The heads of the rushes seemed to nod a slow baseline as the multitude of flashing reflections jumped hither and thither on the water, delivering a staccato melody to entertain the high, midday sun. He recalled that the sun god Ra had been the major deity during certain periods of Egyptian history, and it seemed an eminently sensible choice.

He saw a small patch of clear water close to the bank, and imagined a wicker basket holding a peaceful, sleeping child awaiting deliverance. He was conscious of a certain parallel between Moses and every child of man, for the looming prospect of the undiscovered country has them all awaiting deliverance somewhere deep in their psyches. According to the Bible, Moses grew into greatness, becoming a legendary leader of his people and blessed with the privilege of divine communion. But what value the status of even the most esteemed Patriarch, he thought, when compared with the potential to rise above the god realm and attain joyful oblivion in the universal consciousness. He wondered whether he had muttered his thoughts aloud, for Annie's voice interrupted his musing.

"Well said, Brendan. Are you ready to leave the water now and renew communion with Rabbit and me?"

"Yeah, come on Bren. There are crocodiles in there, you know."

Brendan had forgotten about the infamous Nile crocodiles, and climbed quickly out of the water. Rabbit jumped around and laughed openly; he sensed that Annie was mildly amused.

The riverbank was a mere fifty or sixty feet wide at that point, and beyond it lay a prairie of rippling green. The nearby crops he recognised as wheat, but he could also see stands of fruit trees and bushes a little way off, and another crop he didn't recognise. Those plants looked to be taller than a person, and he asked Annie what they were.

"Papyrus. The Egyptians do a lot of writing, so they need a lot of material to write on. Come on, let's walk."

They strolled slowly along the edge of the wheat field. The plants were still short and green, and leaned slightly as the flow of warm air stroked them. And then Brendan noticed something odd. The stems were bending to the wind behind and ahead of the line of their walk, but the plants immediately alongside the group seemed to stop momentarily and stand rigid, before bending again once they had passed. He assumed it was a trick of the light, some aberration of his own eyesight, or maybe just a coincidence. Annie turned and regarded him with that omniscient look of hers.

"Don't you see that this is my world – the river on that side and the crops on this? You asked me what my job is. This is it: water, earth and seed brought together to generate and sustain life. They will have a good harvest this year, and they will know who helped bring it about. They know me well here, but they have a different name for me."

"Oh really; what's that?"

"That would be telling, but it might interest you to know that there is a connection between Egypt and Ireland, going back much further than the historians can investigate. There is ancient Egyptian blood flowing through the veins of the Gaels. Musicians know it; they hear it in the rhythms and melodic structures. Musicians are among the most powerful of people, did you know that Brendan? They have magic in their fingers, and on their voices. It's surprising how few of them know it in your time. They can manipulate men's heart and minds far more certainly than any great orator. Sound is a great primal force; it can build, alter and destroy, as you'll find out shortly. You sense the magic in music, don't you? I know you do; it's one of the reasons I was drawn to you. I've spoken to you often through your music."

Not for the first time, Brendan was unsure how to respond to such an enigmatic statement. He said nothing. Not for the first time he looked deep into Annie's eyes, and saw something there that caught his breath. No creation of a Michelangelo or Leonardo could come close to matching them for subtlety of meaning and power of expression.

He saw that there were gaps in the crops at regular intervals, narrow tracks that ran at right angles to the riverbank and parallel with each other. They were empty, but he assumed they would be thronging with workers at harvest time. He also realised that there must be a wider road cutting through the field a couple of hundred yards away, for he saw the occasional chariot being driven fast, and heading in the same direction as they were.

"Where are they going," he asked.

"To the pyramid site, the same as us. I said I was going to show you how they were built."

"I'm not entirely sure I want to see it."

"Why not?"

"Because I think I might find the sight of thousands of slaves distressing. I hate slavery."

"Who said anything about slaves? It's true the Egyptians have slaves, but not in the sort of quantity that would be required to build the pyramids by primitive, physical means. Wait and see."

Annie made it clear that she wanted to be quiet for a while. Her two companions demurred to her wish, and Brendan sensed that she had entered a remote mental state, even though her eyes remained open and she continued to walk normally. He further sensed that it had something to do with her spiritual connection to the crops. He was happy to saunter quietly by her side, drinking in the atmosphere of the sunlight, the scent of the vibrant growth, and the comforting babble of the water. This was a flat and fertile land where the balance of earth and the elements seemed in perfect equilibrium.

A boat passed slowly by, its simple fore-and-aft rig consisting of a single sail dyed blue and gold – Annie's colours. Its two occupants had evidently noticed the strangely dressed figure walking alongside the river, for they stared and chattered excitedly. Brendan felt anxious until they had passed. He was sure that Annie would easily handle any awkward situation that might present itself, and yet he still imagined himself a trespasser and was reluctant to be accosted by the locals.

They walked for what seemed like an hour or more, and then Brendan became aware of noise and activity going on a little way ahead. Annie stopped and arrested Brendan by the arm, pulling him around to face her.

"A small adjustment," she said. "You're visible at the moment, so I need to change your vibrations a little. Can you imagine the effect on the people here if they were to see you? A tall man with white skin, dressed like that."

"I'm not tall."

"You are to them. You'll find that most of the men here are several inches shorter than you. Come on, let's get it done."

More nausea, but it was mercifully brief and he was almost becoming used to having his vibrations messed with. He thought he might even miss it when life returned to normal. A pang of regret shook him again as he was reminded that this adventure must end soon and he would have to return to a life that held little of interest, even by human standards.

The field of crops was behind them now, and they moved forward towards an area of flat sand on which many groups of men were working. Blocks of rough stone were lying off to one side of the main area of activity, whilst each group of workers concentrated their efforts on a single block. What surprised Brendan was the strange noise that filled the air. He had expected the sound of hammering and the sharp chipping of chisels on stone. Instead, there was only the drone of men chanting in deep voices, each voice apparently uttering a slightly different note so that the air was filled with a dissonance that he found unpleasant.

"Go and take a closer look," instructed Annie. "They can't see you now."

Brendan moved towards one of the groups and saw that it comprised only six men. Four were sitting to one side and chanting; two more were working on the block with instruments that were unfamiliar. One man sat on one side holding one of the tools steady against the edge of the block. Brendan tried to get a good look at it, but the man's hand obscured much of the detail. From what he could see, it appeared to be made of copper and shaped like a pyramid, with curved geometrical shapes and characters embossed on it in some darker metal like lead. The other man worked on the far side, drawing what looked like a smaller version of the instrument slowly along a straight line. On completing the task, he lifted the uneven top off the block with little apparent effort and discarded it. What was left was a remarkably smooth surface. Evidently, the instrument had sliced the top off the block as easily as cutting balsa wood with a sharp knife.

Brendan's was even more amazed as he watched the two men lift the remaining piece of stone and casually turn it over, where they repeated the exercise on that side. When they had completed the exercise on all sides, they lifted the finely dressed block onto a small wheeled vehicle with remarkable ease. Brendan estimated the block of stone to measure about four feet long, two feet across and three feet high. He turned to Annie.

"What would you say that block of stone weighs?"

"Somewhere between two and three tons. They vary in size. The ones for the bottom of the pyramid are bigger than the top ones; but they're mostly about that weight."

"So how do two men manage to lift it so easily? And what were those tools they were using?"

"Right; the tools are something like what you would call lasers. They harness the power of light. One was projecting a beam through the rock; the other was locking onto that beam and doing the cutting. It makes for very accurate dressing of the stones. But the real magic, if you want to put it that way, is in the chanting. What it does is change the molecular structure of the rock without changing its appearance. It makes it less dense, and so the new structure is less attracted to other bodies. Since gravity is just the mutual attraction of solid objects, the rock becomes lighter. They can vary the degree of change to fine tolerances, even changing it so much that the attraction is removed altogether, and then there's no gravitational pull at all. If they did that, though, the blocks would hang in the air at whatever height they were left at, and then they wouldn't be so easy to transport. It's more efficient to leave them with a little weight so that they can be loaded onto vehicles and carried around. The molecular structure reasserts itself over a few days, and the stones return to their normal weight."

"And is that how it was done in my Egypt, back in my world?"

"What do you think? The details might differ slightly, but the development of technology isn't a straight curve, starting with the stone tools of the cavemen and rising steadily to your twenty first century. Technology has had many peaks and troughs over periods of thousands of years."

"So why did it fall out of use? Why the troughs?"

"Sometimes because civilisations died out and their knowledge died with them; sometimes because jealous new arrivals hadn't the knowledge to use it, and suppressed it for political reasons. The Romans were good at that; they could never tolerate anybody having anything more sophisticated than they did – and plenty of people had such things. If it became known, it would question the superiority of the Empire. The burning of the library at Alexandria wasn't quite the accident people think it was, you know. Shall we go and look at the pyramid now?"

They passed through the work area, and beyond it Brendan could see a massive structure taking shape. He gasped. He had never been to Egypt, and had no knowledge of just how big the major pyramids were. There before him was what appeared to be a gigantic, sloping wall of stone blocks. He estimated its width at several hundred yards, and its height at about that of a four storey building. Vehicles ran back and forth between the building and two sites from which the stones were being supplied. One was the site they had just left; the other was a ragged pile of small, undressed rocks.

"They're for the infill," said Annie. "They've been worked on them for weight, too."

In front of the building, men were engaged in loading both dressed and rough stones into baskets. Other men on top of the wall were hoisting them with the same ease that he had witnessed before; and at the end of the wall tops, yet more men were engaged in using instruments that reminded Brendan of theodolites.

"More laser instruments?" he asked.

"Yes, but more sophisticated. They make for a degree of accuracy that your engineers would marvel at. In fact, they do marvel at it when they study the pyramids."

They walked closer to get a better look at the industry going on, and then strolled to the end of the wall where Brendan saw the same thing happening on the adjoining side. He assumed the four sides were being built simultaneously.

"They'll be starting the entrance passages and chambers next," mused Annie. "That's when things get really complicated."

"The Pharaoh's burial chamber, you mean?"

"It might be used for that, but not necessarily. The main purpose of the pyramid isn't to hold dead bodies, but to harness power."

"From the sun?"

"No, from the subtle energies that they understand and your world doesn't: beneficial energies that help the crops grow, improve the health of the people, and assist the priests in their communion with the spiritual realms.

Talking of which, those men in the blue headdresses are priests. One is a favourite of mine."

"Tell me," said Brendan, "if they were so clever and spiritually advanced, why did they believe the earth was flat and that the sun disappeared into the underworld every night?"

"Oh, Brendan, don't be silly! They only use that image as a symbolic representation of the daily cycle. These people use symbolism much more than the people of your time to understand the workings of the cosmos. They know as well as you do that the earth is a ball orbiting the sun. Your culture draws simplistic conclusions because it fits with what you want to believe – that you are have greater knowledge and are more intelligent than them. You do have more knowledge about certain things, but they were ahead of you in others. And they certainly weren't any less intelligent."

Suitably corrected, Brendan looked around at the busy building site again, and noticed that Rabbit was lying on her side. She looked listless.

"Are you OK, Rabbit?"

"No."

"What's the matter?"

"I'm bored."

"How can you be bored when you're watching history in the making?"

"History? Whose history? Human history? Why would that be of any interest to me? I live outside history, Bren. I'm here for as long as there's a single rabbit on any version of earth. If they become extinct, so will I. The nearest I come to an interest in history is watching the seasons turn, and seeing old rabbits being replaced by young ones. I have no interest in grand buildings, and I really don't like sand very much. The horrid stuff keeps falling on top of you if you try to burrow into it. So I'm bored. But, never mind. We're here for your sake, Brendan my dear old human, and I graciously accept that your education will require the necessity for me to be a bit bored now and then. Aren't you glad?"

Brendan chuckled.

"You seemed to like sand when you were kicking it round with Annie."

"That was different."

"Why?"

"You wouldn't understand."

"I love you too, Rabbit."

"Good."

Brendan expected a comment from Annie, but there was none. He turned back and saw that she was walking towards the group of priests.

"She's gone to amuse herself," said Rabbit, and then closed her eyes again.

Brendan watched as Annie approached the group of men. One of them, a fat little man in a sort of long white kilt, appeared to be in charge. He talked the most and made frequent gestures. When Annie got close to him, he stopped talking, apparently in mid sentence, and looked at the sky. He turned full circle, apparently searching for something. His hands were held tightly together in front of his chest, and he looked excited. He stuttered something to his colleagues and waved them away.

Once they had turned the corner of the wall he resumed his search of the sky and landscape. His face betrayed signs of fear, excitement and desperation; and then he seemed to have been struck a mighty blow. His body shook violently, his eyes closed, and he fell on his knees in front of Annie. His face contorted even more as he opened his eyes and looked up into Annie's face, before casting his head down again. He could have been about to weep, scream, or go into some kind of fit, and Brendan was fascinated by the effect Annie's presence was having on him. She leant forward and touched the top of his head. The priest fell into a position of total supplication and began to tremble. Annie seemed to speak to him briefly, and then walked back.

"I decided to appear to him," she said. "He's a good supporter of mine; one of my favourites. One appearance like that will give him strength for a whole lifetime."

"I don't suppose he saw what I see," ventured Brendan.

"No. He saw a dark skinned, bare-breasted beauty with a golden diadem and braided hair. It's what he expected to see. He will order an image of me to be painted on one of the temple walls, I expect."

"And is what I see more realistic, or is that just what I'm expecting, too?"

"A bit of both, but what you see as my physical appearance will always be mostly an illusion. You can only know me through my actions, the workings of nature, and what you read in my eyes. You're good at reading eyes, aren't you? You always were, and I think you're getting even better at it. Let me paraphrase something I said to you before. Eyes are an illusion; the meaning is real."

Brendan nodded his understanding, and Rabbit hopped over to welcome Annie's return.

"I understand about the eyes," said Brendan, "but I have a physical question. The men here look blacker than I expected."

"Egyptians of this early period were more African than the later ones. Go into your British Museum some time, and look at the statues of the early pharaohs. And now I think we've seen enough and should be moving on. Rabbit's getting bored, poor thing."

"I know. She told me."

They took a shorter route back to the river, bypassing the workmen, and spent most of the walk in silence. Brendan sensed in Annie a reluctance to talk, and then she told him what he had been dreading to hear.

"We're coming close to the end of the journey now," she said with a restrained but unmistakeable look of sadness in her eyes. "I hope it lived up to your expectations; I hope the education was worth some of the bad times you went through."

The axe had fallen, and the pain of its blow was even worse than Brendan had expected.

"So, do I sit the exam now?"

There was a note of bitterness in his voice. In that moment it was unavoidable; he felt bitter, even though he realised immediately that it was born only of regret that the experience couldn't last for ever. He knew that he was being petulant, ungracious and ungrateful. He also knew that it was a common human fault, and that he couldn't help his initial reaction. He was reminded of his feelings as a child on the last day of the summer holiday, or on going to bed on Christmas Day. The joy was ending; the richness and excitement condemned to being nothing more than a memory. He had never subscribed to the view that memory is the means by which things live with us forever. Annie continued.

"Everything is finite, Brendan, and everything is infinite. You mustn't think of this as an ending, but a beginning. From here you will go onto a richer life. The day-to-day routines will be the same, yes. You will continue to eat, sleep, read books, and listen to music; the sun will rise every day in the east and go down in the west; the snow will continue to fall in the winter and the heat bake the soil in the summer; you will get sick occasionally and get well again; life, death and renewal will be a fact of life as it always has been. But you will be different. You mustn't consign this journey to a mere fact of memory, but hold onto the lessons. It's the learning that lives forever. That's what it was about; you must know that, or it's all been a waste of time. You will see the illusion through new eyes, and be better prepared for what comes next."

"Of course I know, and I'm sorry. It isn't just the experiences I'm going to miss, though. It's being with you and Rabbit. I sometimes get an aching sense that there's a big hole in my life, and that it has something to do with living alone and rarely seeing much of people. Mostly it suits me; I'm a natural recluse. But sometimes it feels more like being a hermit; that's too much and it doesn't suit me. I feel held back at the moment - unable to really tell you how I feel about you and Rabbit; I somehow don't feel entitled. That's frustrating. But, if you don't mind me saying so, I'm going to miss you."

"Brendan, do I have to remind you of something you've already worked out for yourself? The reason you're a natural recluse is because, unlike the majority of your species, you're a true seeker. That was an absolute prerequisite when I was choosing who to bring on this journey. And because you're a true seeker, you have to go through life observing rather than connecting in the usual, mundane way. How many people in your life have you felt strongly connected with on a human level? Very few, and – here's the irony – they're all seekers, too. They are your core spiritual group; but none of you are made to get married, settle down, raise a family, and grow old together. Haven't you noticed that those who tried always failed one way or another? Being alone most of the time isn't a curse, as you very well know; it's simply the normal place to be for somebody who's as far along the road as you are."

"I know, but I still get lonely sometimes. That's why being with you and Rabbit was, well..."

He hoped that Annie would make the same simple contact that she had made once before – a stroke of his arm perhaps, or a hand on his shoulder. She didn't; instead he felt a rush of something warm and energising, and yet defiantly impalpable, flow towards him. The contact made his body tingle for an instant, and then it was gone again. They were approaching the river.

"We'll talk more about this later," said Annie. "There's one more thing I want to show you before we go our separate ways. Are you ready for another dip?"

Brendan wanted to say "no," but, of course, he couldn't. He looked at Rabbit sitting at Annie's feet. She had been silent since leaving the pyramid, and was now looking up at him with an expression he would have thought impossible of an animal. It seemed to convey a silent, resigned sadness, much as the look a mother might bestow on a child who is about to undergo an ordeal she has no power to prevent.

"The eyes are an illusion, Bren. The meaning is real," she said quietly.

Brendan knelt before her and fondly stroked both sides of her head.

"Thanks," he said. "That means a lot to me."

And then he pulled himself erect, nodded to Annie, and soon the Great Mother Nile had taken them to her bosom.

Going Home

The trip was over quickly. Brendan was sure that he hadn't lost consciousness at any point, but no sooner had he felt the water rushing over him than his body was arrested sharply and his head broke above the surface.

He was shocked and dismayed at what he saw. He was in the same pool through which he had started his journey with Annie. Every detail was the same: the reeds, the insects, the trees - even the three logs that were still lying at right angles to each other, just as they had been during that first tentative meeting with the farmer, the enigmatic little waif, and her silent animal companion. Annie and Rabbit were already on the bank, waiting for him.

"We're back where it all started," he said. "You said you had more to show me yet."

He wasn't angry this time, merely incredulous and disappointed. He had expected to be taken to another strange world before finishing the journey. This wasn't just his own world, it was only a mile from his own house.

"Do you think I was lying to you, then?"

"No, of course not."

"I'm glad to hear it. Come out of the water and I'll explain."

Brendan realised that he wasn't floating or treading water, but standing on the firm bed near the edge of the pool. He felt silly and exposed, standing like a petulant child in the water while Annie and Rabbit waited patiently. He dragged himself out and climbed onto the bank to look questioningly at Annie.

"Come with me," she said, and proceeded to climb the same embankment that had been his route into the start of his adventure. "You called this place an 'enchanted glade,' I recall. Bit of a fatuous expression, really, but it'll do to describe the place we're in at the moment. Do you remember this?"

They had reached the top of the incline and were standing next to the giant beech tree.

"Of course I do; I could never forget it. It's the tree I was hiding behind when the farmer – or whatever he was – called me down. I remember it well."

"Of course you do, and that's what I'm relying on. Is everything else familiar: the remnants of the wild garlic, the trees with their late summer foliage, the wind in the branches?"

"Yes."

"So where are we?"

"In the copse at the top of the hill, I suppose. No?"

"No. This is a facsimile I'm creating from your memories. It's just another sort of projection; one that I can influence."

"So where are we, actually?"

"I can't answer that, Brendan. You're not sufficiently enlightened to understand it yet. The nearest I could get would be to say that we're where we've always been – in a gap between two adjacent milliseconds. But think about the infinite divisibility of time and space, and you'll eventually get the key to understanding why physical reality isn't real at all. There are no milliseconds; there are only gaps. That's lesson one, something to think about over the coming years."

"Those coming years that won't actually exist, you mean?" said Brendan rhetorically, and with a half formed notion that one day he might understand some of these paradoxes.

"Exactly. Let's walk on and pretend all this is real, shall we?"

They followed the same route back through the wood that Brendan had taken to get there, and everything was precisely as he remembered it. Briefly, he wondered how long ago that had been. Even his own human perception of time had become muddled through the various adventures. He had been asleep or unconscious some of the way; he had even been dead for a while, but he had also seen sunrises and sunsets. Or had he? How could he know? He had been to a place where there was only night. How long had he been in the Hungry Ghost Realm, he wondered.

His thoughts rambled until they became lost in a maze of unfathomable possibilities. Soon, the sense of being in a real place close to his home fell away. Annie had said it was just a projection, and Annie was always right. He tried to consider the question of gaps between milliseconds, and struggled to understand the concept of the infinite divisibility of time and space. He gave up, and fell to merely wondering what it would be like to understand the true meaning of emptiness. His mind wasn't up to working on that at the moment, but at least he realised that there was no point in wondering how long the journey had taken.

They left the wood by the same gap in the old fencing and walked down the same rough pasture towards the lane. The view was exactly right: his own house standing proudly aloof on the opposite side of the lane, the view over the distant valley, the scattered buildings on the high ground beyond the river; every tree and hedgerow was exactly where it should have been. Even the cows were grazing just where he remembered them.

"This is remarkably accurate for a projection," he remarked. "There's no way I could describe this amount of detail with this precision. You say it comes from my memory?"

"Yes. The reason you wouldn't be able to describe it this completely is simply a matter of limited recall. Everything is there inside your head; every scene you've ever witnessed is there."

"Do you see it as I do?"

"Yes, of course. I choose to."

"And Rabbit?"

"Yes. It can only work if we all share the same projection."

"It's nice here, Bren," said Rabbit. "Peaceful. There's a warren over there, by the fence in that field."

"I know; I watch them playing sometimes."

They reached the bottom of the track where the hornbeams and hawthorn grew along the top of the embankment. Brendan shivered.

"This is where I first saw those demons," he said. "They're not still here are they – in some layer of the projection?"

"No, I'm not accessing that part of your memory."

They walked down the lane until they came to Brendan's gate, his house standing a hundred feet away at the top of the sloping garden. His emotions were mixed. The house looked empty, lifeless, mundane; and yet he knew it was safe and comfortable. It was home, and part of him missed it.

"May we go into your garden?" asked Annie.

"Since when did you ask permission to go anywhere?"

"I'll take that as a 'yes.'"

She opened the gate and walked serenely up the path. Brendan followed, watching the elegance of her movement. He wondered how somebody could walk uphill so gracefully. Rabbit had already entered and was nosing inquisitively among the vegetable garden.

"No carrots?" she asked.

"I can't grow carrots. I tried, but the rabbits kept eating the tops."

Rabbits laugh was infectious, and although Brendan had never considered the raiding of his carrots amusing, he chuckled with her. He felt grateful that he had always tolerated the rabbits' inconvenient habit; he fed the birds, after all. Rabbit continued to one of the herbaceous borders, clearly looking for something.

"Thought so," she said triumphantly. "There's a rabbit's bolt hole hidden beneath these flowers. You won't go filling it in when the growth dies off in the autumn, will you?"

"I wouldn't dream of doing such a thing. I'll preserve it always, if only in memory of you."

He felt a sharp pang of sadness again. He had never been good at partings, and this was going to be a bad one. Rabbit showed no emotion at all.

"Good-o," she said, and proceeded to the greenhouse where she peered under the door.

Annie was standing patiently in front of the sitting room window, and Brendan joined her.

"Ready for a bit of magic?" she asked.

"Absolutely. You said you were going to manipulate things."

"No I didn't; I only implied as much. But you're right. Watch this."

The dull scene before him brightened with a suddenness that startled him. It was sunlit, and the sky was devoid of even a single cloud.

"Impressive," he said.

"Right, now I'm going to ask you a lot of questions that will seem eminently pointless, but just stay with me and answer them. OK?"

"Whatever you say."

She held out a finger.

"What's that?"

"A rose bush."

"And that?"

"A leaf."

"What colour is it?"

"Green."

"And what's that?"

"A flower."

"Colour?"

"Pink."

"Good. What's that space called that Rabbit is now frolicking like a mad thing on?"

"The lawn."

"Colour?"

"Green."

"The same green as the leaf?"

"No, not quite. It's lighter."

"And what's that big thing growing on the far side of the lane?"

"A tree."

"What colour is its bark?"

"Dark brown."

"And what's that thing running along the bottom of the tree?"

"The hedgerow. That's green, too."

"What about the elder berries?"

"Black."

"Good. Now let's keep the scene, but change the lighting."

Darkness fell just as quickly as the sunlight had appeared, and Brendan was even more startled. It took his eyes several seconds to become accustomed to it. Annie allowed him the time, and then asked another question.

"Are you still looking at the same things?"

"Yes."

"So do they look the same?"

Brendan considered the question as he peered into the gloom. He wondered what Annie was asking, exactly. His answer was as obvious as he could make it.

"Well, everything is still there, but they're not clearly defined now. The colour's gone; everything is dark grey, some things look black. The tree and the hedgerow form a solid block, silhouetted against the slightly lighter grey behind them. It all looks more one-dimensional."

"So what's missing?"

Another pause for thought.

"The detail, I suppose."

"Right, and that's why some perceptive people say that the best way to see the truer nature of physical reality is to look at it at night. What you see at night is not the separateness of things, but the way in which they are all connected. People are obsessed with individuality, and that's the greatest illusion of all. Everything that appears to exist, be it physical or spiritual, is built of the same energy that has its expression in sub atomic structure; and it's one single, indivisible, flowing phenomenon. It's in the trees, the rocks, the air, every ear of wheat and grain of sand, every insect, bird, animal and human being. There is no state in which you can exist, but that you are connected to every other expression of the universal flow of energy."

"You're talking about chi, of course."

"Of course."

"But there's something I don't understand here. If all material existence is an illusion, why are you telling me this?"

"To explain the illusion."

"The point of which is..?"

"Understanding the illusion is the first step towards sensing it; sensing it is the first step towards seeing it; and seeing it is the first step towards knowing it. Once you know it, you will be able to step out of it. I can say to you 'when everything that is illusion is removed, all that remains is consciousness,' but that won't help the individual raindrop become a part of the sea again. It has to go through the process of being a raindrop first. It has to take its natural course. That's why I said to you once before that you mustn't force your spiritual road. Let the road come to you; just follow the path. Engage fully with the illusion for as long as you're in it. Believe whatever you want, but always be ready to believe something else when that something begs to be let in. Never be certain of anything until you go home to the universal consciousness. Certainty fosters stagnation. As I said before, the certainty of atheism is just as absurd as the certainty of fundamentalist religion. It's the means by which the inherent weakness of the human animal keeps it enslaved. The baby doesn't force itself to grow; it just happens. So it is with your growth towards oblivion."

"So are you and Rabbit just illusions, too?"

"Yes and no. What you see beyond my eyes isn't illusion; what you feel of Rabbit's irrepressible spirit isn't illusion. What you see on the surface is. But we're different than you. You're a product of the illusion; we are part of its mechanics.

"There should be no more questions now. Don't get bogged down by thinking too much about all this. Live your life as you see fit. The seeds are sown and they *will* grow. Just ponder and reflect when the fancy takes you, and let your instinct take the lead. Be open; accept the changes; just be."

Brendan stayed silent, questioning how he felt at that moment. His heart was heavy because this latest speech of Annie's had the tone of a summing up about it, the teacher's final words before the bell rings and the class is over for the day. He didn't want it to be over, but he knew he had no choice and he sensed the rightness of that. A gentle quietness came over him, a mood of acceptance, and with it came an upsurge of energy.

A lot of what Annie was saying had already started to germinate in his awareness, but it had been doing so haphazardly and leaving him frequently confused. Her short speech strung the elements together and made them coherent. It seemed to answer those questions that often came upon him: Who am I? How do I know I exist? What is existence? How do I find out? What should I be doing about it? He could stop worrying about it now. "Let the road come to you; just follow the path." That was good. He felt content to continue the illusion. He looked around the dark landscape and decided he wanted it to be light again. And so it was, instantly.

"Thank you," he said to Annie, "for everything."

She gave him a sideways glance again. It was the one she had bestowed on him whilst sitting quietly on the log by the pool, wearing that kiddie's frock and holding him with those hard, Gaelic eyes - being the enigma. Her eyes were still Gaelic, but the hardness had gone. Now they projected great beauty, maturity and wisdom. Whatever lay behind them was not to be found anywhere else in this imperfect, illusory world; and she was smiling a smile that only a goddess can.

"Hey!" came a complaint from further down the garden. "Who turned the lights on? I like the dark. Rabbits do, you know."

"Blame Brendan," said Annie. "It's his world and he's making of it what he will, as he has every right to do."

Rabbit came dashing up the garden and stood upright, resting her paws against Brendan's knee. That was something else he remembered from that first day. He was struck by how much the world had changed during that gap between the milliseconds.

"What's in your greenhouse, Bren?"

"Nothing much. I only moved here two months ago. There are some young lettuce plants I sowed when I first came in."

"Wow, lettuce! Can I have some?"

"Just because you like the taste, I suppose?"

"Yup."

"Come on, then. For you, Rabbit, anything."

He walked around to the door and opened it. Rabbit hopped in and began to nibble the young leaves enthusiastically.

"Eat as much as you want. Eat the lot, if you like."

"Right," was the brief reply.

"It must be good, being able to talk with your mouth full."

Rabbit carried on nibbling, so Brendan walked back to where Annie had taken a seat at his garden table.

"We have to go back to the pool now," she said. "Do you want to walk back, or shall we take a shortcut?"

"Don't you want to come into my house first?"

"No; it wouldn't serve any purpose. Besides, I've already been in your house. You've even felt my presence a few times, if only you knew it. I needed to study you."

Brendan's small sense of shock kept him mute as he tried to remember having the sort of feelings to which she referred. He'd had lots of odd feelings in that house, but at that moment he couldn't remember any of them.

"So, which is it to be?"

"No point in prolonging things unnecessarily, I suppose. Might as well take the short cut. Dare I ask 'will it hurt?'"

"No, but I do have to put your vibrations right again. I haven't done it since we left Egypt. It will also give my little companion more time to indulge her fancy for lettuce."

She stood up and went through the process. Brendan realised that it was probably the last time she would touch him, and the urge to hold her close was almost painful. He kept his arms dutifully by his side.

"Close your eyes," she said.

He did so and felt his body pressured by the tactile sensation of water. He opened them to find himself submerged and standing on the bed of a pool, clearly the same pool that had been the starting point for his journey. Everything was the same: the plants, the fish, the forest of reeds, the pebbles. He looked up to see the same rippling surface, lit dazzlingly by a high sun; and the nymphs were there, too, clustered among the reeds. Their vague, silver shapes flitted back and forth as before, and their eyes continued to stand out prominently. One thing, at least, was different. They had looked anxious before; now they smiled.

Annie stood before him, and the difference in her was the greatest of all. The waif-like little girl had grown into an image of radiance and beauty that he knew he would never see the like of again. She reached out her hand to him. He took it and they walked out of the pool together.

Rabbit was sitting on the same log that Annie had occupied. She looked a little downcast, or so it seemed to Brendan, and she said nothing. Annie walked over to the log and sat down too. She patted it, inviting Brendan to sit beside her. Rabbit climbed onto her lap and sat looking at him.

"I suppose it's time for the de-brief, is it?" he asked.

"No; I've said all I have to say. No point in repeating myself; but I'm open to questions if you have any."

Brendan felt numb. What could he possibly ask that he hadn't asked already? The lessons had been given, the queries addressed, and now it was time to continue with his life. His future looked bleak in that moment; his acceptance of what was right and necessary was being shaken by the imminence of a parting that would obviously be painful. The pain was already there, settled as a hard knot in his throat. And then the most obvious question of all presented itself.

"Why did you do this? Why did you take me on this journey? What purpose of yours did it serve, and why me? I remember the man saying you wanted me to help you with something."

"Yes, I did; and so you have. I've had a lot of communion with people down the ages; some of it was wholesome, as you would define it, and some of it would probably shock you. There's a bit of the moralist in you, you know, even though you see through that sort of thing. What I never had was a connection with a human that was fulfilling. Let's say I never really engaged with a person, and I decided I wanted to. The problem was my high expectations. The person I would choose had to be somebody I could respect, somebody who had the inherent failings of a human being but who was wise enough to see through them and willing enough to reach beyond them. It needed to be a man, so that I could engage differently than I had done previously with human men. He needed to be sensitive, compassionate, selfless when the need arose, respectful of me, and free-thinking. You were all those things, and I thank you. You might say this was a journey of discovery for me, too."

The knot in Brendan's throat stiffened further, but he stayed strong and resisted the many urges that were making him feverish. He had another question.

"Will I ever see you again?"

"Yes; but I, too, will look different next time. Meanwhile, look for me in every raindrop, in every ear of wheat, in every handful of seed you plant in your garden. Look for me wherever the land and the water meet; part of me will always be with you there. I'll look in on you as well, now and then. I want to do that; I've grown close to you. I'll make sure to give you a little sign, if you're open enough to see it."

Rabbit finally found her voice.

"I've grown close to you, too, Bren. Whenever you see boss lady's signs, look for me as well. I'll be there. Thanks for being a good friend. Keep on loving the rabbits, eh?"

Annie stood up and lifted Rabbit to her chest with one hand. The other she stretched out to Brendan and lifted him to his feet to face her. He felt weak and overwhelmed. He could control his physical faculties, but not the projection of consciousness that left his body, as it had done once before, and rushed out towards Annie. It was not arrested in its course this time.

Once again, time moved into an unfamiliar gear. The first rush of energy slowed to a snail's pace, and he could see it more clearly: a ball of pulsating, golden light that moved slowly but steadily in Annie's direction. And then he saw something similar emanating from her. It was bigger and brighter, and flashed with sparkling fragments of blue, yellow and green. They met in the space between their two bodies, and there was an explosion of light so vivid that Brendan became temporarily blind. And with the light came a tingle that started at the base of his spine and moved swiftly up to his head, gaining in strength until it lifted his consciousness clear of his puny body. A sense of sublime madness engulfed him immediately, a certainty that nothing mattered any more. Nothing existed except the euphoric, orgasmic joy that was as far removed from ordinary experience as the sun is from a grain of sand. An inner eye, even more deeply set than the one he had used before, held an image that would be impossible to describe or reproduce. It was an image of Annie, Rabbit and himself as one reality: nothing and everything. He fell to his knees, shaking violently with the power of it all.

And then the light faded as rapidly as it had come. Deep darkness descended on his sight and his very being. He opened his eyes and it lifted gradually, revealing a flower-bedecked space containing a pool with three logs at one end. He felt the sunshine on his skin and heard the rustle of the breeze in the branches. This was it. Annie and Rabbit were gone. It was time to go home.

Acceptance

Brendan stood up and surveyed the scene through washed out eyes. Never had he felt such a sense of being abandoned and alone. He knew it was just a first reaction to the shock of sudden parting; he was still human, after all. He decided not to try unscrambling the cocktail of emotions that were pressing in on him at that moment: the opposing forces of joy and despair, the gratitude for the unique experience he had been given, the wonderment, the sense of disbelief. They could all take their course with the due process of time, however much it was now indelibly inscribed that time is but one of many illusions.

He walked up the slope of the bowl until he came level with the beech tree. He turned to take another look at the scene below him. He smiled sadly when all he saw was a shallow depression filled with the same remnants of summer growth that clothed the rest of the woodland floor. That, at least, was what he had expected. And he also saw the true scale of the copse. That's all it was, an inconsequential collection of trees and no bigger than a football pitch. He could see the edges of it in all directions and made for the nearest point of exit.

The view from the top of the airy upland swept over the same panorama that he had looked at only a short while before. All the detail was the same, apart from the fact that the cattle were a little higher up the slope. The August sun still shone high and proud, and the light breeze stroked his skin. He saw and felt everything as a normal human being should. He even felt hungry. Normality had been re-established, even though the unquestioned nature of reality was gone forever.

The ache of emptiness persisted, nevertheless. Much of the substance of his inner life seemed to have been plucked out and cast away, like weeds from a neglected allotment. Some healthy crops remained, and new seed had been planted to fill the gaps. They would grow in accordance with their own directives, unhurried by undue effort on his part. He must be content with that, however low he felt at present. He made his way across the lea, down the track, and through the gate that accessed the lane.

He groaned when he saw a group of men approaching from the direction of his house. There were three of them, two walking side by side talking amiably, and one walking a few paces behind. He had learned that it was a common sight on the quiet lane at the bottom of his garden. They were ramblers, and the pattern of rural lanes and public footpaths made a popular destination for people wanting a few hours of undemanding exercise in the peace of the countryside. He had learned, too, that they liked to stop and pass the time of day. They would comment on the beauty of the landscape, tell him how they envied the fact that he lived in such a delightful spot, congratulate him on the stolid charm of his Edwardian house, and offer the predictable lament that modern houses are so plain and dull by comparison. Brendan wasn't in the mood to engage in pointless small talk; he wanted to hurry past them with a polite nod, and seek the solace of his home without further delay.

The first two offered no problem. They were still engaged in their own conversation as he reached them, and they were content to return his polite nod. One of them grunted an incoherent greeting, but they made no attempt to slacken their stride. The third man was not so accommodating. He had been making a more comprehensive observation of the surroundings, looking up at the tree branches, following the flight of a bird across the road, and taking a prolonged interest in the copse on top of the hill. He stopped as Brendan approached, and offered a smile that seemed a little more familiar than the forced version usually given to a stranger who just happens to be passing by.

"Good day to you, sir," he said with predictable enthusiasm. "Fine day for a ramble in strange territory. I wonder if you could help me."

Brendan had an inbuilt need to be polite – something bred into him as a child, he'd always supposed. It could be inconvenient at times, and it was inconvenient now. He felt stung by the innocent irony of the man's statement, and his first instinct was to say "not today I can't," and walk on; but he resisted it as he always had. He suppressed the impatient, irritated groan that was desperate to be given free expression, and stopped to wait for the question.

"Is there a public footpath up to that copse on the hill?"

Brendan's annoyance swelled even further. He had developed a strong proprietorial bond with that copse. Only he belonged there; it was a sacred place; he didn't want anyone to go near it ever again; but he remained polite and pushed away the feelings that he knew were childish and unreasonable. He pointed to the gate a hundred yards along the lane, explaining to the man that it wasn't strictly a public footpath, but that it led only to some rough pasture land and nobody would object to their presence. He warned him that there were young bullocks in the field, and assumed that it wouldn't be a problem as they were peaceable enough. He privately hoped that the walkers wouldn't want to enter the copse, but made no reference to it.

"Oh, right," replied the man, "only I've been told there's a pool up there and I wanted to take a look at it."

The mention of the pool sent a shock through Brendan. A sense of suspicion followed, and he looked at the man for several seconds as he sought a rational explanation. And then he remembered having been told about a pool by someone from the village.

"Oh, I see," he said as the simple revelation explained the mystery. "You must mean the heronry. I've never been there myself, but I gather it's about half a mile beyond the crest in the direction of the main road. Follow a line towards the farmhouse you'll see on your left, and I expect you'll find it."

"That's odd," continued his inquisitor. "I'm sure I was told it was in the wood. Are you sure there isn't a pool in there?"

Brendan's suspicions returned. Why would this man be so set on the question of whether there was a pool in the wood? Who had told him it was there? And he thought he noted something unusual about the man's manner. A knowing look about his eyes and an unusually benign smile suggested that he wasn't actually questioning, but making a point of some kind. Brendan put the impression down to the mood he was in, and his impatience to get home.

"Quite sure," he said decisively. "I've just come from the wood, actually, and there definitely isn't a pool in there."

"Would you know whether there's ever been a pool there?" continued the man, the same mask-like expression settled on his face. "Maybe it dries up in the summer, eh?"

The way the man uttered the interrogative "eh" sent another shock through Brendan. It sounded familiar, and he wondered...

"Oh well, I'll walk up there and take a look for myself. Must be off. Thanks for your help."

With that, he turned and followed his two companions who were now some way ahead. Brendan watched as the leading two walked past the gate without even looking at it. The third man unbolted the gate and walked through it. He waved to Brendan as he slid the bolt back, and then walked on, soon disappearing beneath the line of hawthorn and hornbeam on the raised field edge. Brendan turned to walk homeward, but stopped again when he heard a deep, rich laugh issue from that direction. Only one person he had encountered in his whole life laughed like that. He thought of chasing after him, but decided against it. He felt weary. If the rambler was just a rambler, there would be no point; if Brendan's suspicion was correct, there would still be no point. This man, or being, or whatever he was, appeared and disappeared according to his own agenda. He wasn't to be chased. Brendan moved on and completed the short walk to his gate.

As much as he now felt ready to re-enter the comforting familiarity of his house, there were two things he wanted to check first. He walked over to the herbaceous border where Rabbit had pointed out the bolt hole. He was delighted to see that it really was there, and vowed never to fill it in. But then a thought struck him. The facsimile had supposedly been constructed from his own memory. If he hadn't known about the bolt hole, how could Rabbit have seen it? He thought about it for several minutes, and then assumed there must be a rational explanation. Maybe he had noticed the hole, but failed to register the fact. Or maybe there was really no such thing as a rational explanation. Was this another lesson left as a legacy, he wondered. He decided to let the matter resolve itself when it was ready. Let everything take its own time; that was the new principle by which he should be guided.

He walked to the top of the garden and looked through the greenhouse window. He was disappointed to see that the young lettuce plants were all there too, but he realised it made sense this time. Rabbit had eaten the facsimiles; the originals would be untouched. He unzipped the pocket of his coat and took out his door key. He assumed it would work perfectly, and it did.

His house felt chilled, as though it hadn't been occupied for some time. He should have expected that; he had remarked often enough that the ground floor of the house was often cooler than the outside in summer. He looked at the clock sitting on top of the fireplace. 2 pm, it said. He turned on the TV to check the date, and his expectations were confirmed. It was now about an hour after he'd originally left the house to walk up the hill. He wondered why he felt hungry if he'd only had lunch an hour ago, and wished Annie was there so that he could ask her. He had become used to Annie knowing everything and explaining it all to him. Standing alone in his cold living room, a pot of gloss paint sitting on the dust sheet folded in one corner of the floor, and a set of stepladders standing next to them, the memory of Annie and Rabbit seemed all the more poignant. He wished he had something tangible as a keepsake of that long, magical moment between the milliseconds; and then he remembered the copper pebble.

He pressed his hand impatiently into his pocket, his fingers pushing aside the various bits of useless paraphernalia that should have been discarded long ago. They lighted on a hard, round object and he pulled it out anxiously. It was just a sea coal fossil he had picked up on a beach some years earlier. He searched again. He ransacked all his pockets, emptying each one of them onto the hearth rug until they were all empty of everything but bits of fluff and sandy detritus. There was no doubting the fact; the copper pebble wasn't there.

To Brendan's current state of mind, this was a devastating blow. Annie had said he could keep it and bring it back to his world. It was the only proof that his journey had ever happened. Did he need proof, he thought. He struggled with that one. He had lived every moment in apparently real time, and yet the clock had only advanced one hour, about as long as it took to walk to the wood and back again; and he had been repeatedly shown that reality isn't what it seems on the surface. So didn't that very showing constitute evidence in itself? He didn't know; he couldn't be certain of anything. But then, he wasn't supposed to be certain of anything; Annie had said so.

His mind was in a heady state of confusion and he felt on the verge of slipping beyond sanity. And then the confusion cleared. There was no question that the journey had happened, just as there was no question that his fifty two years of life on this planet had happened. They might both be illusions, but they had both happened. If one constituted some form of objective experience, so did the other. He was content with that, and assumed the pebble must have dropped out of his pocket somewhere along the way. That depressed him, but he would get over it.

He went to the kitchen to make a sandwich and a cup of tea. He took them out into the garden and sat in the same chair that Annie had sat in. But, of course, it wasn't the same chair; that one had been merely a facsimile. And then he noticed that his stomach was aching with tension. He rested his elbows on the table, buried his face deeply into them, and gripped the top of his head tightly. He let out a long, agonised groan, and then ate the sandwich.

He sat there all afternoon, feeling the peace of his isolated location, revelling in the sunshine, and watching the birds flitting busily to and fro. He tried to convince himself that the robins, the blackbirds, the sparrows, the dunnocks, and all the rest were not individuals at all. He was only partially successful, but it was a start. When the rose red disc finally settled itself behind the copse on the hill, he felt it was a sign to put his thoughts away until tomorrow; tomorrow he would carry on painting. Today had been fuller than any day in the life of a human had a right to be, and he was immensely weary. An early night seemed the proper way to end it.

Epilogue

The rest of August was chilly and changeable with frequent periods of showery weather. That suited Brendan, since he wanted to concentrate on the decorating work. There was no hurry to get the garden into shape; that could wait until next spring.

It was more time-consuming than he had expected. The preparation work seemed to go on interminably – so much filling, sanding, dealing with chipped paintwork, scraping the many layers of emulsion off the power sockets and switch plates. The speed at which he had earlier painted the window frame soon proved prematurely optimistic; the rest was a long way short of being ready for top coats. The work was, however, just what he needed in the circumstances. It was mostly mechanical, and allowed plenty of opportunity to muse on the strange episodes he had witnessed and the things Annie had said to him. His mood lightened gradually as he saw his physical effort making a difference, and the living room and study were completed around the middle of September.

A fine Indian summer had descended, and Brendan decided he would take an extended break. The sun was no longer high in the sky, but it still offered plenty of warmth on the still, mellow days of early autumn. The leaves were showing the first hints that the season was advancing, the willow herb was clothed in its feathery froth, and the broad view over the quiet and peaceful valley looked like a painting by some Italian master. He sensed the softening of the earth energies as nature began settling herself to sleep.

He started to take daily walks around the narrow lanes and along the public footpaths. He explored the many woods in the vicinity, discovered several quaint buildings, and made casual enquiries about the old mill, the disused railway station, the dilapidated remains of a cricket pavilion, and the medieval church. None of this seemed to have any relevance to advanced spiritual learning, but that didn't matter. He was taking each day at a time, living his life in the world that surrounded him, and accepting that the road would come to him when it was ready. The one place he never went to was the copse at the top of the hill. He didn't want to go there for some reason. He didn't know why, but the prospect made him uneasy. Maybe he simply feared the disappointment he might feel on seeing that nondescript depression in the ground.

Breakfast, lunches and dinners were mostly taken at the table standing at the top of his lawn and giving a view of his own little kingdom and the wider world beyond. He grew to love the spot; it connected him with Annie, and he frequently stared at another spot – the one in front of his window where she had stood. It was a comfortable, restful place; any passing guilt at his voluntary idleness was always quickly dismissed. He dozed occasionally, read a lot of books, and began to keep a journal; and so his days continued for two uneventful weeks.

It was 30th September. The weather forecast had promised another fine day, probably the finest in the present spell of supremely clement weather. He was in no particular hurry to begin it. It would be another lazy one; the beneficent sun and the gods of the elements gave him all the permission he needed. There would be time enough to start the autumn clearance work in the garden when the chill winds arrived, and the rest of the decorating could wait until the winter rains encouraged him to stay indoors.

He took his breakfast al fresco as usual. He looked at the sky as he munched his cereal, and felt content. There was no sign of a cloud in the rich blue sky. The weather forecast had been entirely accurate. He remembered other coloured skies that he had seen on his journey, and the blue dress that the child Annie had worn during that first trip through the water. He felt a keen pang of loss again, but brushed it away. Life has to move on, he thought, and then muttered "Whatever that means." He went to the kitchen to make a pot of coffee, and returned with a steaming mug and the local newspaper.

He looked at the sky again, and was surprised to see a dark grey cloud drifting with apparent purpose from the north west. He thought it strange, since there was no wind; and it seemed singular somehow, drifting alone in an otherwise clear sky. His eye was caught by a movement a little way down the garden. A full grown rabbit came hopping out of the undergrowth, taking up a position at the edge of the lawn and staring into the distance. He had seen this several times, and had discovered that the animals were quite content to sit there as long as he didn't move. He remained still and watched. And then the rabbit did something that none of the others had: it turned its head and looked at him. It was not a momentary glance of curiosity, but a full blown stare that lasted several minutes. Brendan felt a growing sense of recognition as he stared at the animal's eyes. He began to feel excited, but cautioned himself to circumspection.

"Rabbit?" he said quietly.

The rabbit continued to stare at him, and Brendan decided to stand. If it was Rabbit, she would welcome him. If it was merely a wild creature, it would bolt as soon as he moved. It bolted, and Brendan shrugged inwardly. The sun was still shining in the south eastern sky, and he had forgotten the cloud that had approached from the opposite direction.

The downpour was unexpected and comprehensive. By the time he reached the protection of his kitchen, he was soaked. And then he heard a familiar giggle, or thought he did. It seemed not to come from any external source, but from inside his ear. It was brief, and shortly afterwards he heard the torrential rain cease. He looked out on his sodden garden, and heard the water rushing down the spout and gushing noisily into the grid. The urge to go back to the copse hit him like a mild electric shock.

He changed into dry clothing and donned his walking shoes. Within ten minutes he was striding up the rough pasture of the lea. The animals were gone now, and the crown of the copse was flecked with patches of yellow. He entered by the same piece of broken fencing as he had on that glorious, fateful day in August, and followed the same route to the depression at the far end.

What he saw surprised him. It seemed the third rambler might have been right. The depression must have lain on bedrock not far beneath the surface, for it was boggy. There was no single pool there, but the heavy shower had left many large puddles in its wake.

He looked at it fondly and imagined an unbroken body of water, until he saw something gleam in one of the puddles close by. He reached into it and pulled out a shining copper pebble. Another near lapse into insanity followed, but he remained sensible and told himself he must have dropped it on his way home. That didn't stop him muttering a heartfelt "thank you," and the two little words triggered a brief bout of sobbing that spluttered unashamedly through his helplessly smiling face.

He sat by the beech tree for the rest of the morning. The whole wood seemed to be smiling Annie's smile, and no amount of sense was going to make it appear otherwise. Eventually he felt hungry and decided to go back.

On his way home he began to plan another journey. He wanted to go to Ireland and find that cottage near the lough again. He felt a thrill as he wondered what he might see on the walk along the lane. Might it be that his inner eye would be better attuned than it had once been, or might the occupants of the wood somehow contrive to make their presence felt? Rabbit had indicated that he would see them again, and he had no reason to doubt that they would remember him.

The main reason for the trip, however, was to visit the Rafferty family. He knew he would have to contrive a reason, but felt confident that he would think of something. He counted out nine of his fingers, and decided that the end of May would be about right.

www.ingramcontent.com/pod-product-compliance
Lightning Source LLC
Chambersburg PA
CBHW071701090426
42738CB00009B/1618